Picasso on a Schedule

The Art and Science of Managing IT

Stephen K. Wiggins, CIO

and

Kenneth C. Abernethy, PhD

ISBN: 1463772807
ISBN 13: 9781463772802

Library of Congress Control Number: 2011913485
CreateSpace, North Charleston, SC

Picasso on a Schedule

The Art and Science of Managing IT

Contents

Part II: Enabling Client Value

Part III: Creating Client Value

Acknowledgements

In writing this book, we have benefited from the help and support of numerous people, because the ideas captured here are distilled from a great many experiences and thoughtful conversations. Colleagues who have shared those experiences and engaged with us in those conversations will no doubt see their influences within these pages.

But there have been so many of these experiences and conversations that we would be certain to leave out important contributors if we tried to recount them all by name. And so, with apologies for not mentioning all of you, and with the assurance that the absence of names doesn't mean we are any less in your debt, we sincerely thank the following groups.

The intelligence, dedication, and hard work of the management team and professional staff of the Information Systems Division at BlueCross and BlueShield of South Carolina have produced the incredible success story on which much of the material in these pages is based, and we offer sincere thanks to all for your remarkable efforts. To all the participants of the IMIT Summer Institutes at Furman University, we thank you for your openness to learning, your willingness to engage in meaningful discussions, your cheerful endurance of "Summer Boot Camp," and your thoughtful feedback on how the institute experiences could be improved.

Of course, those great learning experiences were also the consequence of our able and dedicated institute faculty, and so to the faculty of the institutes goes our sincere thanks for your professionalism, enthusiasm, preparation, insights, as well as your own willingness to learn. The support staff, both at Furman and in the

I/S Division, have worked tirelessly to make the institute experiences as rewarding as possible, and we thank all of you for that.

Finally, while the contributions of these groups have been invaluable in helping us formulate, revise, and refine this material, we take sole responsibility for any and all errors and misrepresentations that might have survived the final edit.

Steve Wiggins and Ken Abernethy

Preface

The purpose of this book is to explore a set of concepts that we believe are fundamental for the management of information technology (IT) as a successful business. The ideas and concepts explored here have emerged from a ten-year collaboration between the authors in creating professional development programs to support and enhance the remarkable success of a particular IT company—the Information Systems (I/S) Division of BlueCross BlueShield of South Carolina. However, the book is about more than one company's success. Indeed, it is our hope and belief that anyone facing the challenge of managing an IT company, an IT unit, or IT projects of most any size will find ideas and concepts here that resonate with their experiences and that will provoke them to think in new and more productive ways about the work they do.

For the purposes of this book, *information technology (IT)* is defined to include three major components or areas. First, IT traditionally involves the study, design, development, implementation, support, and management of computer-based information systems. Second, these systems typically enable the converting, storing, protecting, processing, transmitting, and retrieving of data for one of two major purposes: (1) *data processing*, which turns data into useful, meaningful, accessible information; and (2) *process automation*, which controls machinery and/or processes to reduce the need for human sensory and mental intervention in work. And third, IT can be thought of as the formation of a collection of *products*, comprising computer hardware and/or software; and *services*, including telecommunications hardware, software, and services.

At a more general level, and following the U.S. Bureau of Labor Statistics categorization, IT can be considered as a distinct industry comprised of IT-related companies as well as IT organizations or companies within other industries (a "business within a business"). As a business within a business, IT can then be viewed as an important subset of manufacturing, transportation, banking, insurance, business services, and other sectors.

To run IT as a business and gain business competence, IT professionals must be exposed to and institutionalize the common practices and governance under which non-IT businesses operate. However, an obsession with running IT like a business can distract IT professionals from technical operations. Running IT as a business is a critical step in achieving IT *efficiency*, but IT professionals are also responsible for making IT *effective*. This is achieved through a focus on technical competence. The key, of course, is to properly balance efficiency and effectiveness. We believe the concepts presented in this book enable such a balance by offering IT professionals the ability to maintain and support the creativity necessary for excellence, while imposing appropriate structure and controls to ensure a balanced focus on technical and business competence.

In addition, we hope this book will help in educating business software users and purchasers so they might have a more realistic set of expectations about software, software development, and the delivery of information technology as a service. Through this new knowledge, we ultimately hope businesses will understand why they cannot control the data processing and process automation required to run their business efficiently and effectively without the help of IT professionals.

As we have noted, the ideas explored here have emerged from a ten-year collaboration between the authors in creating professional development programs to support and enhance the success that the Information Systems (I/S) Division of BlueCross BlueShield of South Carolina has experienced over the past several decades. This success has been impressive. The division operates as a business within a business in the context of a family of insurance businesses. Since the early 1990s, the division has sustained steady growth, evolving from an organization of 300 people to one employing more than 2500 people, and increasing the total number of annual online healthcare transactions from just under 700 million to over 14 billion.

Many of the concepts explored in this book have been in place in the division for much of this time, while some have been put in place more recently. Through a process of adaptive change, all are continuously monitored and modified or enhanced when needed. The underlying principles discussed here have been articulated and refined as part of an intensive eight-day Summer Institute for the Management of Information Technology delivered at Furman University to I/S Division managers, project managers, business analysts, infrastructure experts, and software developers. Since 2004, more than twenty such institutes, averaging more than twenty participants each, have been conducted.

In each chapter we have defined and discussed general concepts, ideas, principles, and processes that we believe underlie some of the I/S Division's major success factors. These ideas have proved essential to the division's success, and we are confident that they can contribute to the success of any IT company or any internal IT organizations supporting companies in other industries. Where appropriate, we offer brief examples that illustrate how the central ideas have been successfully applied. We would be pleased to provide more details about our experiences with these ideas for those who are interested.

While it is not the intent of these examples to elaborate the complete application of the concepts within the I/S Division, they do offer a "proof of concept" that these ideas are applicable and have in fact been important in a very successful IT company. We believe that they can also provide insights into possible ways they can be used to advantage in other environments. Indeed, beyond these examples, our main hope is that the IT professionals reading this book will find their own advantageous applications and adaptations of these concepts, and we welcome feedback about these experiences.

For the busy professional who wishes to sample the ideas before delving into the entire case presented for them in the book, we have provided an "executive summary" in Part V, where the main ideas are laid out in outline form with guidelines for their practical application. This summary will also serve as a convenient and quick review of the central ideas of the book.

Part I
Building a Framework for Success

Chapter 1

Introduction:
The Art and Science of Software

The programmer, like the poet, works only slightly removed from pure thought-stuff. He builds his castles in the air, from air, creating by exertion of the imagination.

Frederick P. Brooks, Jr.

Whether an information technology (IT) organization's mission is the creating, maintaining, executing, or hosting of self-created systems; the selecting, installing, executing, or hosting of vendor-supplied systems; or some combination of the two; at the heart of every computer system is the software that supports the specific requirements of a given user. There are two major challenges facing an IT organization: One is the identification and use of operational and administrative processes that the IT organization must perform to produce a desired outcome. The second is the identification and use of basic IT roles that must be successfully fulfilled as they relate to these processes. We believe that to truly understand these challenges, one must understand the fundamental nature of software and its development.

Software development has long been recognized as a complex combination of art and science. Frederick Brooks [1] makes this point eloquently in his essay "The Tar Pit," in which he describes both the joys of creative work, and the woes of working to satisfy the external demand for perfection that the computer hardware imposes on the programmer's creative efforts. Donald Knuth's [2] classic multivolume work on the tools and techniques of program and algorithm creation is aptly titled *The Art of Computer Programming*. On the other hand, attempts to focus on the science and engineering aspect of software development are behind the current use of the term *software engineering*. And while efforts to move software development toward an engineering discipline represent an admirable goal, we believe they also include a substantial portion of wishful thinking. Indeed, the dichotomous nature of the craft of software development—part art, part science—has led to many misunderstandings and misconceptions in both the software user/purchaser and IT communities.

A "thing" like a bridge or building has a natural sequence of construction dependencies in the physical world that a person can observe and imagine easily, so it is not too difficult for that person to form an intuitive understanding of the product as well as the construction process that produces it. Software is not a thing. Business people who are not programmers have a hard time understanding what software really is because a software product is entirely abstract, and there is no physical-world frame of reference to allow an intuitive understanding of the product and its associated construction process.

This lack of a physical frame of reference leads to misconceptions among business software users/purchasers, producing an *understanding gap* between them and IT professionals. For example, users/purchasers often perceive that software development takes ten times longer than they think necessary. They tend to believe that creativity can and should occur at *warp speed*, and that just adding people to work efforts decreases development time. They also envision IT systems that are fully featured and complex and do everything anyone could want on day one of their implementation.

Driven by the media hype associated with much new technology, software users/purchasers also expect systems that take full advantage of ongoing technology changes and that are always technically current. And finally, users/purchasers are accustomed to employing a network of computers (and other IT devices, like smartphones) that can seemingly produce instantaneous information, answers, and connections. Hence, in their worldview, these expectations of new and modified IT systems are the norm and thus they have little appreciation of the inherent challenges that producing these represents for developers.

At the same time, IT communities, in an attempt to provide an intuitive understanding of the software construction process and the products themselves, have focused on the science and engineering aspect of software development to help mitigate some of these misconceptions. Unfortunately, we believe that by not including the "art component" of software development in the attempt to explain the nature of software, the understanding gap is only widened.

The underlying reality is that software and its development embodies both art and engineering. We believe that recognizing and accepting this inevitable dichotomy are the first steps toward effectively managing information technology and toward educating software users/purchasers to better understand software products and their construction processes.

To more readily accept the art and science reality, consider some of the similarities and differences between the craft of the artist and that of the software developer as shown in table 1.1. The similarities demonstrate that software development does indeed have elements that make it a creative, even artistic, process. However, the differences have important implications for the potential of managing the software development process—while at the same time demonstrating the difficulty of managing in the usual sense the traditional artistic endeavors.

First and most importantly, both the artist—we use this term generically to refer to a painter, sculptor, composer, novelist, or poet, among others—and the software developer are engaged in a highly creative process. Both set out to create abstract representations of underlying realities that can never be completely and unambiguously specified. The work of each is in essence a work of the human imagination. Each creates something out of "nothing," in the sense that they work with and produce abstract representations.

Table 1.1
Art and Software
Summary of Similariaties and Diffferences

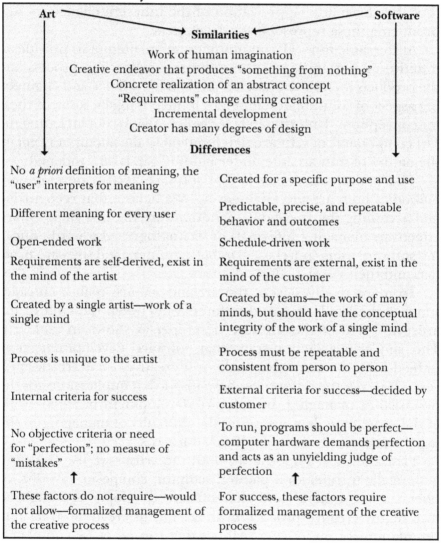

Art		Software
	Similarities	
	Work of human imagination	
	Creative endeavor that produces "something from nothing"	
	Concrete realization of an abstract concept	
	"Requirements" change during creation	
	Incremental development	
	Creator has many degrees of design	
	Differences	
No *a priori* definition of meaning, the "user" interprets for meaning		Created for a specific purpose and use
Different meaning for every user		Predictable, precise, and repeatable behavior and outcomes
Open-ended work		Schedule-driven work
Requirements are self-derived, exist in the mind of the artist		Requirements are external, exist in the mind of the customer
Created by a single artist—work of a single mind		Created by teams—the work of many minds, but should have the conceptual integrity of the work of a single mind
Process is unique to the artist		Process must be repeatable and consistent from person to person
Internal criteria for success		External criteria for success—decided by customer
No objective criteria or need for "perfection"; no measure of "mistakes" ↑		To run, programs should be perfect—computer hardware demands perfection and acts as an unyielding judge of perfection ↑
These factors do not require—would not allow—formalized management of the creative process		For success, these factors require formalized management of the creative process

You could perhaps argue that the painter and the sculptor do in fact employ tangible materials, but in fact the artist drastically alters the states of those materials to create something that was at best only an implicit abstraction in the artist's mind at the beginning of the work. Like composers, software developers use no tangible materials at all to create their desired products. In Brooks' term, they create pure "thought stuff." Although the software developer uses computer hardware to demonstrate the created product, just as a composer will want to hear a composition played on tangible musical instruments, these devices and instruments are not the raw materials of the creative product but are rather channels for the tangible realization of purely abstract concepts.

There are other similarities between the work of the artist and the software developer. Both strive to satisfy a set of "requirements," although as we will see shortly, the source and nature of these are quite different for the two. Additionally, they both typically employ incremental development methods and techniques. Neither the work of art nor the computer program emerge fully formed from the minds of their creators but evolve through an iterative process of creative trial and error. And this creative trial and error process is made even less certain and more unpredictable by the range of creative freedoms both the artist and the software developer have in choosing a design for the form and features of their end product.

People engaged in highly creative processes tend to exhibit resistance and even defiance when presented with the structured and disciplined management of these processes. This observation is as true for software developers as it is for artists. However, there are some essential differences between the crafts of art and software development that ultimately lead those working in the two domains to respond differently to structured management. These differences make it both necessary and possible to effectively manage the software development process, although this management should always be tempered by an awareness of the similarities we just discussed.

The most important difference between art and software development concerns the underlying motivations for the respective creative efforts. Art typically has no *a priori* meaning or uniquely specified purpose. For example, consider the painting *Still Life with Guitar* by Pablo Picasso, reproduced as part of the cover of this book. It would be naïve and futile to try to describe it's "meaning." The meaning of a work of art is in essence created by a person when he or she experiences the art. The meaning derived and defined by this experience is highly subjective and differs, perhaps quite drastically, from person to person. The uniqueness of each person's perspectives and life experiences contribute to and become a part of this meaning.

In contrast, software is always created for a specific purpose and use. Objective criteria are applied to assess whether or not the software lives up to its intended purpose. More specifically, software is judged by its behavior on computer hardware, and this behavior is not expected to be different for each user. Indeed, software is expected to produce precise, reliable, and predictable behavior and outcomes when it is run; if it does not, its failure to do so will be obvious to all involved parties.

In other words, there are always external objective criteria to judge the success of a software development effort, whereas the success of an artistic endeavor is evaluated subjectively by both the artist and those experiencing the art. This has implications for the degree of management required in these two creative domains. We must manage the software development effort toward the objective criteria of usefulness and purpose that gave rise to the effort in the first place. A successful software development effort produces a product of value that is recognized and accepted by all users.

Of course, appropriate boundaries must be put in place to guide the creativity and contain the schedule, costs, and the degrees of freedom software developers employ in their craft. Such guidance and containment would likely be unwelcome in the art domain, and if we made such an attempt, creative disagreements would abound and be difficult or impossible to resolve because of the lack of any objective criteria for success. But it is the existence of objective success criteria that forms the basis and rationale for our effective management of software development efforts.

In fact, the software we develop must not only succeed in the purpose or use for which it was intended, but it must also achieve a standard of internal perfection that has no equivalent in any other discipline. This "perfection requirement" is imposed by the hardware on which the software is instantiated. Programs that are 99.99 percent correct can fail in spectacular ways when they are run on the target hardware—indeed they can fail to run at all! There is surely no analogy to this for works of art, which are evaluated subjectively. A "perfection requirement" is therefore impossible to define and holds little meaning even if we attempt to define it.

Another important distinction between the creation of art and software is that software creation is *always* conducted within the constraints of a clearly specified schedule and budget. Artistic work is most often more open-ended, especially with respect to schedule. The creative processes of the artist are typically characterized by the unpredictable nature of the muse. Artists are noted, at least in the typical stereotype of popular culture, as temperamental souls whose work simply cannot be rushed and placed on a schedule. Whether this perception fairly characterizes the majority of artists or not, it does result in a certain tolerance for the time it may take to complete a work of art.

An example of this, though admittedly on the extreme end of the spectrum, is the case of the Crazy Horse Memorial project. In 1939, the noted and acclaimed sculptor Korczak Ziolkowski, who had worked on Mount Rushmore under Gutzon Borglum in 1924, was contacted by several Lakota tribal chiefs about the possibility of creating a similar monument to Crazy Horse, one of the great Native American heroes. Ziolkowski accepted this challenge and began the process of choosing an appropriate site for the monument.

Slowed by the Second World War, the work to carve the sculpture did not actually begin until 1948 on a mountain just a few miles from Mount Rushmore. The monument is a nonprofit undertaking, and receives no federal or state funding. Ziolkowski was offered $10 million from the federal government on two occasions, but he refused the offer both times because he felt that accepting the funding would result in too many constraints on the direction of the project. Ziolkowski died in 1982, and the project has yet to be completed, although work on it has continued to this date—see figure 1.1. An important milestone was reached in

1998 when the face of Crazy Horse was completed and dedicated. The sculpture's final dimensions are projected to be 641 feet long and 563 feet high, which would make it, if completed, the world's largest statue.

Figure 1.1: The Crazy Horse Monument (partially completed).

Of course, it is quite clear that a sixty-year software project would be unacceptable to most organizations. But as important as schedules are in the craft of software development, these are rarely central to the efforts of the artist. The reader can imagine the possible results of placing Pablo Picasso on a schedule to create *Les Demoiselles d'Avignon, Guernica, Three Musicians,* or any of the host of other masterworks he painted. Yet software development organizations routinely ask highly creative people to meet demanding schedules every day.

In addition to adhering to more structured schedules, software development is also more constrained by costs than most artistic efforts. The main driver of software cost is labor, and the work of software development is usually done by a team. Managing the logical complexity of a large software product, ensuring that it meets the objective criteria of its requirements, and testing it for correctness and quality requires the expertise of multiple persons. Indeed, writing the code itself is usually a team effort and typically requires the largest concentration of people within the project. On the other hand, art tends to be the work of a single mind or at most that of a small team, and though there are exceptions, costs are not typically a primary driver in an artistic endeavor.

The very nature of requirements is another distinguishing feature between art and software. The artist's requirements—*parameters* may be a better word—are largely self-derived; they exist primarily in the mind of the artist who will implement them. By contrast, software requirements are not self-derived, but come rather from the mind of the customer. Therefore we need a robust, repeatable process to discover, articulate, and validate software requirements, whereas in art all this is accomplished by processes that are created and deemed appropriate by the artist at the time.

Indeed, essentially all of the artist's processes are—or at least could be—unique to the individual. Techniques may be borrowed, learned, or adapted from other artists, but the ultimate decisions about which processes to employ are all made by the artist. There is no external need for standardization or validation of processes, which can be changed or abandoned as quickly and as often as the artist desires. On the other hand, software development processes are usually governed by a set of standards and definitions that the supporting company has found to be successful through its experience and its knowledge of industry best practices. Standardized processes are necessary for good communications on projects, for auditing project work, for reporting purposes, and for organized meaningful quality assurance methods. The organization must ensure that its processes are suited to their intended purposes, well understood by those carrying them out, and produce similar results when employed by different persons trained in the processes.

Finally, as we have noted, the work of the artist is usually the work of a single mind. By contrast software development projects of any significant size are done by teams and are often modified by different teams over time. Hence these are created by many minds, but in this process care must be taken to maintain the conceptual integrity of the software so that it appears to emanate from a single mind. In this way, the software can be more readily enhanced and maintained over time by different individuals without compromising its quality and purpose. Obviously, accomplishing the goal of perceiving the conceptual integrity of a single mind within the work of many minds requires a great deal of coordination, communication, and a focus on common design principles. And this process must be properly managed to ensure its continuity and consistent application.

To formalize the management of the creative process of software development, there are three basic IT roles that must be fulfilled as they relate to operational and administrative processes: *management, programming,* and *technical support.* The scope of these roles as well as further specialization of these roles is based on the level at which IT administrative and operational processes are implemented within an IT organization, which is in turn a function of software use, technology complexity, and IT organization staff size.

This book is about the challenges of managing IT organizations. Of course, such organizations are required to manage a host of supporting functions and processes necessary for success—acquiring and maintaining infrastructure, developing/acquiring and maintaining the software products themselves, ensuring excellent customer service and support, and incorporating appropriate changes in information and computer technologies.

Many of the challenges we will discuss confront non-IT organizations as well, but as we will see, the nature of the creativity involved in virtually every IT work effort presents some unique challenges. Indeed, the art and science of managing IT organizations demands its own highly creative as well as highly developed and repeatable approaches to successfully accomplish the organization's work. In many ways it is the equivalent of putting Picasso on a schedule to create a masterpiece using a specified amount of effort, within a specified time period, that will satisfy a specific art lover's definition of a work of art, and can be purchased at "starving artist" prices.

Chapter 2

Evolution, Not Revolution: Achieving Sustained Improvement

I don't look to jump over 7-foot bars: I look around for 1-foot bars that I can step over.

Warren Buffett

Much has been written in the past decade about the importance of innovation, agility, and change in creating and sustaining successful organizations. Agility can be defined as an organization's ability to sense changes and to adapt efficiently and effectively to them. In an economy marked by rapidly changing events and business assumptions, the ability to sense and understand change, and then respond to it in an effective way, becomes an essential survival skill.

Peter Drucker, who has written extensively about innovation and change, declares that it is a central twenty-first-century challenge that organizations become change leaders. [3] These organizations see change as opportunity and actively seek out the right kind of change for the organization. While we might be tempted to assume that such organizations would embrace bold and daring steps to establish themselves as change leaders, in this book we argue that the best process for doing this is an evolutionary as opposed to a revolutionary one.

In his book *Good to Great,* Jim Collins found evidence of the value of an evolutionary approach to change. His study of companies that rose from good to great revealed no pattern of singularly identifiable, transforming moments to which these companies could attribute their remarkable success. Instead, Collins found evidence of the transforming impact of combining and adapting existing ideas in innovative ways. He concluded that while revolutionary leaps in results were evident, these were not achieved by the revolutionary process of creating drastically new and different ideas and concepts. Instead, he found that evolutionary, not revolutionary, processes were at work in achieving successful change. [4]

Perhaps no industry is more acutely aware of the challenges of living with rapid change than information technology. In this chapter we gain insight into how IT organizations can use an evolutionary approach to change in order to achieve process and product innovation that leads to sustained improvement.

Becoming a Change Leader

Changes in the IT industry come from a variety of sources, the primary ones being rapid advances in hardware, software, telecommunications, and the associated customer expectations. Attempting to manage or retain control over changes of the magnitude we have seen in these areas over the past thirty years is futile. But if managing change is not possible, can IT organizations become change leaders? Can they learn to position themselves to be in front of important changes instead of being swept aside by the current? We believe that IT organizations *must* become change leaders to survive.

How then does an organization go about being a change leader? Most importantly, the organization must use an analytical and systematic approach focused on creating continuous improvement as the primary basis for becoming a change leader. The organization must be willing to change—modify, replace, or eliminate—what is already being done, indeed perhaps change what has been most successful for the organization, more than depending on creating completely new and different directions. The organization must make an honest assessment, which involves examining successes as well as failures and problems. In fact, it may well be that within the organization's current successes lie the seeds of the great break-throughs of tomorrow.

Using an evolutionary approach to change involves being able to sense change and respond efficiently and effectively to it by see-ing the right kind of change as an opportunity. Determining the right kind of change involves adopting a willingness to change by regularly making a skeptical examination of each product, service, client, market, technology, and distribution channel. When any of these are not producing value for the organization, they should be modified or, if necessary, replaced. In this effort, the change leader organization should be willing to regularly examine the value of its strategic directions as well as its implementation pro-cesses and methods. When the value of a work effort doesn't justify its cost, the organization should eliminate it and focus its resources elsewhere—a process Drucker refers to as *organized abandonment*. Despite the phrase, organized abandonment is an evolutionary, not a revolutionary, process.

An analytical approach to a continuous evolutionary strategy of change can be greatly enhanced by a framework for making the necessary environmental scans—both internal and external. The Information Technology Organizational System Design (IT-OSD) model illustrated in figure 2.1, which is discussed in chapter 3, pro-vides such a framework. As shown here, the model has three main component groups: external influencing factors, organizational choices, and results of these choices in the form of culture and out-comes achieved. As organizations respond and adapt to new environ-mental challenges, the model provides a framework that captures the interconnections and interdependencies inherent in any complex organizational system, enabling organizations to take these intercon-nections and interdependencies into account when design choices are made.

Externally, the model provides a framework to ask, and the awareness to provide reasoned answers to, questions like the following: What new challenges are our clients and their customers likely to face in the future? How are our competitors positioned to respond to these challenges? What weaknesses in our current products and services—and the organization knows these better than anyone if it takes time to reflect on them—are likely to be exposed by these evolving challenges? What IT industry realities and best practices impact our processes, products, and services? How can these realities and best practices be accommodated to make our organization stronger and better positioned for implementing positive change?

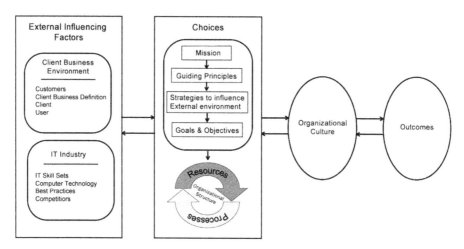

Figure 2.1: *The Information Technology Organizational System Design Model.*

The model also provides a framework for productive and meaningful introspection, by articulating the nature of the organization's core elements—guiding principles, strategies, goals, and objectives—and the underlying resources, processes, and organizational structures that enable the outcomes the organization produces. By considering possible new or modified outcomes that might be required by changing future business environments and developments within the IT industry, the model allows the organization to undertake an integrated analysis of what organizational design choices might need to be modified to achieve such outcomes.

This analysis, if acted on, leads to systematic, gradual, continuous improvement. The IT-OSD model is designed to facilitate organizational renewal, which should be driven by the expectation of improved products, services, performance in efficiency and effectiveness, and processes. Improvement implies change, and the model helps the organization assess its capacity for the required change and align its design choices to optimize its accomplishment.

The Nature of Innovation

Sustained improvements over time lead naturally to process and product innovations. Systematically anticipating and proactively responding to change is closely aligned with innovation. An innovation is more than a brilliant new idea; it is accomplished by creating something new that *also* proves to be appropriate and useful for some purpose. Indeed, we believe that most of the time an innovation does not involve "brilliant" new ideas at all. Rather, innovation results from a creative combination of existing ideas, concepts, and products in ways that spark new products and services, although sometimes one can be fooled into confusing the attributes of being clever or novel with those of being innovative.

Andrew Hargadon explores the idea of innovation as systematic work in *How Breakthroughs Happen*. Based on ten years of study into the origins of historic inventions and modern innovations, Hargadon's findings reinforce that innovations do not usually result from flashes of brilliance but are much more likely to come about from the creative combination of ideas, concepts, and products from existing technologies—a process Hargadon calls *technology brokering*. [5]

In an interview after the release of his book, Hargadon described the application of these ideas. He emphasized the importance of continuity and its critical role in the innovation process:

> By focusing on recombining existing ideas—rather than inventing new ones—we can better exploit the sources of innovation and, at the same time, increase the likelihood of their impact. It's much easier to think of things that have already been done and, when you introduce those ideas into new markets, they are already well developed. The trick is putting yourself or your firm into position to be the first to see these opportunities. Highly successful firms have developed a set of innovation strategies, called *technology brokering strategies,* that enable them to move between different worlds, to see how ideas from one market's past can be used in new ways in another market. [6]

Hargadon endorses the idea of letting the present create the future. He captures the idea even more succinctly with one of the several "rules" he discusses in the book: *the future is already here.* In other words, organizations that seek to anticipate and exploit change do well to consider carefully the activities, products, and services on which they and others are focused. It is almost always the baseline of present activities that allows organizations to make the insightful moves that position them as change leaders in their industry.

Another of Hargadon's rules—*analogy trumps invention*—provides practical advice on how to go about using the present to create the future. First, focus on recombining existing ideas rather than inventing new ones. This approach has more promise simply because it is easier to recognize the similarities between two situations than it is to come up with something no one has thought of before. This approach replaces searching for insights and flashes of brilliance with the more promising approach of looking for successful ideas and inventions in other areas and thinking creatively about how to combine them, modify them, and apply them to the opportunity or problem at hand. Second, overcome the false assumption that the problem being tackled is unique, has never been studied, and has never been solved in any context. Instead, assume there is a good chance that someone somewhere has tackled an analogous problem and crafted a solution to it even though it is not exactly in the context in which you are dealing.

Looking for appropriate analogies requires adopting an open mind and cultivating the ability to employ *lateral thinking*, to use the term coined by Edward DeBono. Lateral thinking means *thinking inside other boxes* instead of following the more common advice of thinking "outside the box." The usual meaning of *thinking outside the box* challenges us to create something new and different— unrelated to any approach used before. While this happens once in a great while, it is more common and productive to pull ideas from "other boxes" that have proven successful in other applications and combine them in creative ways to address the issue at hand. [7]

The preceding discussion has shown that an IT organization is usually better positioned for success if an evolutionary approach to change is used to achieve process and product innovation. The question now is how does this lead to achieving sustained improvement for the organization? The answer lies in three basic tenets: (1) leveraging success; (2) expecting and being receptive to the unexpected; and (3) balancing change and stability.

Leverage Success

When conducting environmental scans to identify and anticipate potential change, it is important to focus attention on successful efforts as well as those that are experiencing difficulties. Successful change leader organizations focus on their best opportunities. While opportunities can emerge from problems and difficulties, they often originate from within the organization's successful products and services. For example, there may be opportunities to enhance a product or service, expand its scope and market, or leverage it to produce a successful new product or service in a related area or with another client.

It is easy for any organization to fall into the trap of focusing its best resources on its outstanding problems rather than its best opportunities. But the organization that does this is unlikely to become a change leader because their best talent is not being used to anticipate and respond to the changing environment. This can be penny-wise and pound-foolish in light of the potential differences in payback between solving problems and exploiting new opportunities. Of course, problems cannot be ignored, and some problems take on the character of crisis and demand, at least for the moment, the attention of the best minds the organization has. But the change leader organization measures carefully the resources, both in quantity and type, that are applied to problems versus those that are applied to the systematic review and analysis of the organization's successes with an eye toward leveraging or improving these efforts. Continuous improvement and innovation require the best thinking an organization can mobilize.

Expect the Unexpected

Once we anticipate a change and craft a response to it, how should we proceed? First, it is important to acknowledge that when we implement something novel, it is unlikely that we'll get it completely correct right out of the gate. Part of the work of innovation is correcting the bugs and refining the focus, even if the underlying idea is fundamentally sound and valuable. So, we should expect the unexpected to happen. When a new idea does not turn out to be successful, we must be open to trying something a little different, going in a slightly different direction, or even making major adjustments to the concept and its application. To create solutions of value, a constant assessment of the current state of a product or service against customer requirements and demands is a critical success factor.

These inevitable adjustments are another reason that the evolutionary approach almost always works better than the revolutionary approach. With the evolutionary approach, the organization might naturally consider an appropriate venue to *pilot* any new developments. The use of a pilot project has several advantages. First, it is on a small enough scale so as not to interrupt the entire organization if it fails outright—which is always a possibility. Second, even if it doesn't fail, it is likely to need further improvements before it becomes a success. Making the requisite improvements is much easier when the initial effort has been clearly identified as a pilot. People expect pilot projects to require some tinkering and fine-tuning, and it comes as no great surprise even if major modifications are required. Within the context of a pilot, this additional work can proceed in a more orderly and deliberate way than if the new product or service had been rolled out to the whole organization at once.

Another advantage of a pilot effort is that it provides a relatively low-risk opportunity to explore additional applications of the new concept. One of the unexpected outcomes may be that the idea fails to achieve its stated objectives but leads to a different objective. For example, the process of trying the original idea may produce new insights that could lead to a different use or opportunity that may have otherwise gone unnoticed.

To realize these kinds of benefits, those involved with the pilot effort must resist becoming overly invested in the *current version* of the concept and its application, leaving themselves open to considering additional and perhaps far more significant applications of the concept. Indeed, often a proposed new product, service, or technology finds its major market and its major application in places the innovator and entrepreneur may not have expected. This, of course, can only be discovered by trying out the original novel product or service, then modifying it based on what is learned. This cycle may even be iterated several times before the final successful application of a concept is found—clearly an endorsement for an evolutionary piloting process.

In summary, once a response has been created to anticipated change, an IT organization should be open to the reality that the response is unlikely to be completely correct out of the gate. Perhaps the best strategy for discovering what types of adjustments may be needed to create an ultimate success is to use the technique of piloting solutions as a vehicle for implementation.

Balancing Change and Stability

Organizations achieve success by becoming change leaders, but the people who work in them thrive on continuity and stability.

How then does the organization find and achieve the proper balance between change and stability? This balance can be delicate indeed. Too little change can leave an organization obsolete, out of touch, and fighting to maintain its existence; too little stability can produce chaotic working conditions, weaken investor confidence, and scare off customers, making it difficult to retain the talent, capital, and market share needed for success. Finding the proper "sweet spot" is no easy proposition.

The key to maintaining the proper balance is to separate the elements of the organization that can and must change to enable success from those elements that should be more stable over time, changing more slowly and deliberately. Again, the IT-OSD model can guide these considerations. In the middle portion of the diagram illustrating the model (figure 2.1) are listed the various elements that represent design choices for the organization. A number of these choices are elements that are fundamental to the organization as it is currently conceived—its mission, guiding principles, and basic business strategies. These represent the core characteristics of the organization.

All of these core characteristics are dynamic and may change over time, but they typically change slowly and deliberately over a fairly long period, as indicated in figure 2.2. When these elements do change rapidly, as they might in a corporate takeover, an IPO, or the purchase of a private company by outside interests, the likely outcome is a disoriented chaotic work environment. This outcome can produce high turnover, poor morale, reduced productivity, and a host of other organizational pains. However, when an evolutionary change process is being used, it is uncommon for the core characteristics to change at a rapid pace.

On the other hand, the organization's more specific strategies and its goals and objectives, while typically stable over reasonable periods of time, may shift noticeably during a period of evolutionary change. The processes, organizational structure, and resources needed to implement evolutionary changes may exhibit even more rapid change. The understanding of just what design elements might change and the effective communication within the organization of this understanding are crucial factors in maintaining the proper organizational balance between change and stability. If people in the organization understand that the organization's mission, guiding principles, and basic business strategies are stable, they have a rudder to use in navigating the necessary changes.

Elements Apt to Change	Elements More Stable
Specific Strategies Goals and Objectives Processes Organizational Structure Resources	Mission Guiding Principles Basic Business Strategies

Figure 2.2: *Nature of change of IT-OSD design elements.*

Evolutionary Change and the Business of IT

Thus far, we have examined the general argument that an evolutionary approach to innovation and growth is preferred over a revolutionary approach. There are additional factors specific to the business of IT that reinforce the advantage of an evolutionary approach to change and growth. These include certain IT realities that should be taken into account by any company seeking to create sustainable competitive advantage using IT.

Nicholas Carr has argued that IT had become so commoditized that its contribution to competitive advantage is in question for most companies. It is largely true that the technological infrastructure of IT has become a commodity. Companies typically purchase off-the-shelf hardware in order to assemble their technical infrastructures. As a consequence, it would be difficult to achieve a competitive advantage primarily through infrastructure. Furthermore, some categories of software have become commodities—office productivity software, accounting software, operating systems, communications software, and enterprise resource management software to name some specific categories. It seems unlikely that any company could achieve a competitive advantage using such standard and common software on standard infrastructure components. [8]

However, we believe Carr's argument does not recognize the constant efforts to absorb and integrate information technology to enhance productivity and expand market opportunities that many companies employ. Carr's argument focuses on the design and development components within our definition of information technology that can and do produce commoditized IT components. However, it ignores the implementation, support, or management of computer-based information systems that leverage the help of IT professionals to manage the data processing and process automation required to run a business efficiently and effectively. We believe management of IT as a successful business or a business within a business, by IT professionals responsible for making the organization both effective and efficient, does provide an opportunity for IT to contribute to the competitive advantage of the companies it supports. The IT-OSD model described earlier can provide a means of analyzing the degree of competitive advantage IT can contribute.

In addition, the design and development components of IT can still apply to an important category of software that has the promise of providing competitive advantage. A great many business areas can benefit from *customized software* to enable their employees and, if applicable, their customers, to engage more effectively and efficiently in the company's business activities. Thus, highly tailored software that performs complex core functionality within business application areas has the potential to create a competitive advantage if it is properly constructed and deployed. The software that accomplishes this typically embodies a depth of business intelligence as well as algorithmic solutions of considerable logical complexity. The creation and maintenance of such customized software requires a depth of knowledge and experience in both IT and the underlying business, and its development is often difficult and always highly labor-intensive. Its complexity can reach daunting levels as both the depth of embedded business intelligence and the intricacy of the software's internal logic grow over time.

What strategies would be appropriate for producing this type of software? Complexity—both of the embedded business intelligence and the internal logic—is the central feature of such software that permits the realization of a competitive advantage. It is this complexity that makes it difficult to replicate the software and thus permits companies the time to recover the considerable costs of its development and go on to reap benefits from it. Of course this same feature also makes the software difficult and expensive to produce in the first place, and hence the software development strategy must be carefully chosen. The complex nature of the software is even subtler than it might first appear; the complexities of the business intelligence it captures and the logic of the code itself are intertwined. Business intelligence is dynamic, and hence regular enhancements are necessary to keep the software current. But these enhancements are not usually designed as self-contained modules, and must be integrated into the existing code, producing considerable additional complexity in the overall software system.

In a sense, the business intelligence and the software "grow up" together, and the complex synergies that are created in this process are designed at different points in time. In other words, the evolutionary nature of the development and modification of the underlying business intelligence all but *forces* a corresponding *evolutionary development strategy* for the software that instantiates it. The only other choice would be to completely redesign large complex systems on a regular basis—a process far too expensive to be practical.

Hence the use of an evolutionary development approach in customized business software is often as much a *constraint* as it is an organizational design choice. But nonetheless, it serves to create value for the organization because the resulting evolution of system complexity generates the "flywheel" effect that Collins discusses in *Good to Great*. The metaphor of the flywheel focuses on the inertia of the wheel. It is difficult to get it moving, but once in motion it gains momentum and is difficult to stop. This suggests how difficult it might be for a competitor to duplicate the effort required to create such a complex system, and hence such a system erects an effective barrier to competition.

We should note that the potential for competitive advantage for the kind of software we are discussing is inextricably connected to the value of the embedded business intelligence in the resulting system. As a consequence, for the evolutionary approach to produce its intended strategic value, there is an essential requirement. The IT organization must develop and maintain strong client relationships to cultivate the mutual trust needed to give it access to the necessary business intelligence. As we discuss in chapter 3, this kind of trusted relationship can produce substantial benefits for the client as well as the organization. Further, by its very nature the cultivation of strong client relationships is itself an *evolutionary* process.

There are important strategy and design choices that the IT organization *does* make in this process. Among the most important of these should be the choice to embrace an intentional strategy of conducting incremental development within a strong system-design environment in order to preserve the conceptual integrity of the system and make it possible to effectively manage its increasing complexity. As we show in chapter 4, the system architecture is a major factor in these considerations, and it should be designed and nurtured with these purposes in mind.

A well-known example of the failure of a revolutionary approach within the IT industry illustrates how indispensable the evolutionary development of meaningful client/IT relationships can be. The period from 1985 to 2000 was characterized by revolutionary change in the IT sector. By the late 1990s, the hype for the complete redefinition of business by the Internet and e-commerce reached a crescendo. Internet and Web technologies, coupled with the increasingly ubiquitous availability of computers and Internet access, appeared set to enable businesses to make unprecedented revolutionary leaps into the future. Brick and mortar businesses were being advertised as endangered species in a wide array of business areas, ranging from furniture sales to grocery delivery to legal services.

Internet-based companies formed rapidly and attracted huge funding almost as soon as they came into existence. Existing companies rushed to add an "e-" prefix to their name, sparking a corresponding advance of their stock price in what Michael Masnick [9] called "prefix investing." The typical "dot-com" company's business model focused on operating at a sustained net loss to build "market share," which did not mean a group of paying customers but rather awareness and visibility within potential markets. The theory seemed to be for dot-com startups to get big as fast as they could as measured by brand awareness, with the hope of making a profit for their services later. As an example of the strategies that emerged to attempt this, advertising for Super Bowl XXXIV in January 2000 included seventeen dot-com companies, each of which paid over two million dollars for a thirty-second ad spot. During their non-revenue period, these companies relied on venture capital funding and the enormous amounts of capital raised through initial public offerings to tide them over.

Of course, we all know the end of the story. The so-called "dot-com bubble," which reached its apex in March 2000 when the NASDAQ peaked at more than 5,000 points, was soon to be renamed the "dot-com bust." The revolution didn't happen the way it was predicted. The revolutionary approach ignored the necessity of the evolutionary building of business partnerships and the evolutionary nature of the practice of innovation. Eventually, e-commerce did gain traction, and we can now point to companies like Amazon, Google, and Netflix that have become spectacular successes. But those successes took time and followed a more traditional evolutionary development path, learning from mistakes and practicing the processes of continuous improvement.

As an even more recent example of how inappropriate revolutionary approaches can be for many businesses, consider the collapse of the financial sector during the latter part of 2008. The rapid embrace of financial leveraging instruments like derivatives and mortgage-backed securities that promised to revolutionize the investment industry, in the absence of adequate understanding about their long-term implications, led to a severe global economic crisis. Once again, a more evolutionary approach, which would have allowed the incremental assessment of some of these implications and the development of corresponding correction efforts and controls, could have perhaps helped the financial institutions avoid much of this economic pain.

Evolutionary Change in IT: An Example

As noted in the Preface, many of the examples in this book reflect the experiences of the Information Systems (I/S) Division of BlueCross BlueShield of South Carolina. The division is an organization of approximately twenty-five hundred people. Its role within the company is to provide and support the IT systems—both infrastructure and software systems—that enable that company's various health insurance-related businesses. A second major role is to generate revenue for the company through offerings of back-office services and claims processing for other healthcare payers, including both government and commercial organizations. In fulfilling these roles, the division operates as a "company within a company."

Since the early 1990s, the division has refined an evolutionary approach to sustained growth and innovation. The factors that have resulted in the organization's success have evolved over time as the organization has systematically explored strategies to enable adaptive change consistent with its perceived strengths. Over this time frame, the organization has either embraced fully, or adapted as appropriate, proven concepts and associated techniques to implement these strategies. In addition, the organization has developed guiding principles supporting evolutionary growth through the integration and alignment of processes, resources, and organizational structure to produce desired outcomes.

The division's approach to growth and innovation embodies specific applications of many of the principles of evolutionary change we have explored. The evolutionary approach was chosen primarily because it offered an excellent and natural fit for the capabilities and opportunities on which the organization has been able to capitalize. In other words, it was the approach that *worked*, and in applying it, the organization discovered many of the associated underlying principles that define and reinforce its value.

The organization's growth plan was based on what might be called an *organic growth model.* By this we mean building growth based on existing core-business models and capabilities as opposed to seeking growth through entirely new products or services that might be obtained by the creation of completely new lines of business or by acquisition. The organic growth model can be naturally implemented as a directed evolutionary strategy.

With this approach, the organization has experienced the steadily increasing operational volumes since 1993 that we cited earlier—representing a sustained annual growth rate of almost 20 percent for more than fifteen years. This growth has come about by pursuing the evolutionary expansion of the scope of business capabilities within an integrated system architecture. This expansion has been designed to accommodate important external factors and realities in both the client business environment and the IT industry.

Naturally, supporting such growth in capacity has required a corresponding increase in division staff—increasing from 300 people in 1993 to more than 2500 by 2010—an annual growth rate near 14 percent. Importantly, the evolutionary development approach has provided the ability and opportunity to implement a smooth integration of this substantial additional staff over time, while ensuring the basic stability of the organization's mission, guiding principles, management philosophies, and fundamental administrative and operational practices.

Chapter 3

A Model-Based Framework:
The Information Technology OSD Model

Rational behavior requires theory. Reactive behavior requires only reflex action.

W. Edwards Deming

The pursuit of a strategy ensuring the value customers expect must be intentional and provide the context for decision making across the organization. While all organizations would acknowledge the importance of the connection between strategy and desired organizational outcomes, realizing this connection can be difficult. The challenge, of course, is to understand and articulate the appropriate mission, create strategies that can enable the accomplishment of that mission, and implement those strategies through processes and people to produce the desired results.

Understanding the complex nature of large human organizations is never easy. One of the most productive approaches to doing so adopts the underlying premise that organizations are in essence complex systems. W. Edwards Deming takes this view of organizations and defines a system as "a network of interdependent components that work together to accomplish the aim of the system." He offers a good orchestra as an example of a well-optimized *system*—interconnected components collaborating in complementary and well-synchronized ways to produce an outstanding result that is bigger than the sum of its parts. Deming asserts that most problems in any organization can be attributed to the system of the organization. "In my experience," he writes, "most troubles and most possibilities for improvement add up to proportions something like this: 94 percent belong to the system (the responsibility of management); 6 percent are attributable to special causes." [10]

For our purposes we define an organization's *system* as the framework the organization uses for decision making supported by the interconnected network of processes that provide the organizational infrastructure that enables the actual work of the organization. The challenge to understand organizations could then be rephrased as the challenge to understand an organization's system and its subcomponents that must be integrated to support the work, decision making, accountability, adaptability, and flexibility necessary for the organization's overall success. Borrowing an approach from the sciences, complex systems can perhaps be best understood through the use of system *models* that abstract the most important features of a system as well as their codependences and interactions.

The IT-OSD Model

Paul Gustavson phrased the essence of this challenge for all organizations (non-IT as well as IT organizations) when he observed that "every organization is perfectly designed to produce the results it gets." [11] The key word in this observation is *designed*, and there is an immediate conclusion we can draw from this: to change results we must modify elements of the organizational design. Seeking to simply change what people do without making design changes to the system is unlikely to produce the desired modifications in results. Too often we take this approach and look to heroic efforts from outstanding individuals to correct deficiencies and create better results. The preferable alternative is to create systems that enable extraordinary results to come from the dedicated but ordinary efforts of people.

Gustavson developed the Organizational System Design (OSD) model to help organizations better evaluate and understand the connections between various organizational design factors. We adapted Gustavson's model and introduced the IT-OSD model in chapter 2. It is reproduced in figure 3.1.

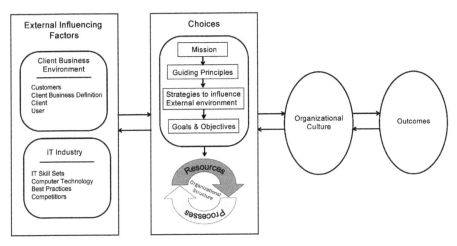

Figure 3.1: *The Information Technology Organizational System Design Model.*

The IT-OSD model, as its name suggests, takes a system view of the organization. The model captures at a high level the most important design elements inherent in any IT organization—external influencing factors, choices, and results in the form of culture and outcomes achieved. We submit the model as a framework for an evolutionary and systematic approach to the development and implementation of an IT organization's administrative and operational practices that facilitates continuous improvement.

IT External Influencing Factors

External influencing factors, of course, vary over time. While the organization may have little or no direct control over these influences, it can nevertheless make design choices that help to accommodate the impact of these external factors relative to the organization's ability to achieve its desired outcomes. Note that the IT-OSD model groups important external influencing factors for an IT organization into two broad categories: the *client business environment* and *the IT industry.* Each of these categories represent outside elements that directly affect the nature of the results created by an IT organization.

Client Business Environment

The client business environment is comprised of the IT organization's clients, the clients' business definitions, their customers, and the users of the systems the organization produces. A client is anyone who purchases IT products or services directly from the organization. For a particular client, the client business environment is defined by the buying and selling of goods and services by that organization in support of *its customers.* Understanding this business environment requires knowledge of the client's short- and long-range business plans, financial plans, organizational structures, and current business practices and operations.

The client's customers are the persons or businesses that purchase a commodity or service offered by the client. A user is any person who uses IT services for activities related to the client's business. Other important aspects of the client business environment are the regulations and laws within which the business operates and the various parameters for their application. In a similar way, government entities with which the client does business can have powerful influence also. Where this situation applies, an understanding of a government agency's goals, objectives, and accountability to its stakeholders positions the IT organization to create better value in the products and services it sells to its clients.

The IT Industry

The IT industry is both a distinct industry and a subset of manufacturing, transportation, insurance, business services, and other industries and sectors, according to the U.S. Bureau of Labor Statistics. Thus an IT organization is a part of the very industry that is the second broad category of external influencing factors that an IT organization must consider. This second broad category comprises four components: (1) providers of computing technology—hardware, software, and communications infrastructure; (2) the marketplace availability of IT skill sets required to support computing technology utilized by the IT organization; (3) IT industry best practices, which offer various frameworks for computer systems development/maintenance, operations, and management; and (4) the organization's current and potential competitors. Just as with the client business environment, it is important to know to the extent possible the impact changes in the IT industry can have on your organization's, as well as your competitors', capabilities and offerings.

Gaining knowledge about relevant technology providers can be enhanced by scheduling regular meetings, conference calls, on-site visits, or formal training sessions and by attending trade shows to keep abreast of technology. Conducting regular reviews with technology providers focused on upcoming activities associated with their specific technologies helps an IT organization anticipate important relevant developments, and performing technical interviews and analysis with a technology provider can help the organization determine the road map or life cycle associated with its specific technologies.

Of course, the market availability of IT staff needed to support an organization's technology is of crucial importance. Information about this availability can be acquired by conducting compensation studies to determine IT skills categorization by job descriptions and salary ranges within the marketplace.

Awareness and knowledge of IT industry best practices can be obtained by monitoring leading professional organizations, associations, and consortia that articulate and publicize frameworks in computer systems development, maintenance, operations, and management. One such resource is the Information Technology Infrastructure Library (ITIL) project, which offers some of the most widely accepted resources for IT management in the world.

The ITIL is published in a series of books, each of which covers an IT management topic. The names *ITIL* and *IT Infrastructure Library* are registered trademarks of the United Kingdom's Office of Government Commerce, which uses the ITIL to distribute regularly updated best practices in IT management, based on expert advice and input from ITIL users. The library is both current and practical, combining the latest expert thinking with sound, common sense guidance. The volume on IT Service Management has become a particularly popular resource in the management of IT infrastructure and the delivery of excellent IT service.

Another major resource of best practices for the software industry is the Software Engineering Institute's Capability Maturity Model Integration (CMMI), a certification process that focuses on providing organizations advice and recommendations on the essential elements of effective processes. The principles embedded in the CMMI certification are intended to guide software development process improvement across a project, a division, or an entire organization. Among the primary goals of CMMI is to encourage and help organizations integrate traditionally separate organizational functions, to ensure that they set and assess process improvement goals and priorities, to supply guidance for quality processes, and to provide a point of reference for appraising current processes.

Over the past several decades, project management has become increasingly recognized as a critical discipline within the software development industry. With well over 250,000 members in over 170 countries, the Project Management Institute (PMI) is the leading membership association for the project management profession. In its *Guide to the Project Management Body of Knowledge*, the institute offers the most accepted embodiment of project management best practices in the world, and its Project Management Professional certification is a globally accepted credential. [12]

Of course, it is also important to know your competitors' capabilities and offerings. Keeping abreast of the offerings of various technology providers can provide insight into developments your competitors may be using or considering. Another way you can gain knowledge is by knowing your clients' business environment.

In fact, the specific competitors, products, and services that you need to track most carefully are the ones that are likely to appeal to your clients. Careful analysis of the client business environment can provide insight into relevant competitor activities.

Design Choices—The Heart of the Matter

Between external influencing factors, and culture and outcomes stands a range of important design choices that the organization makes—some explicit, some perhaps implicit. As figure 3.1 suggests, these design decisions are related. The most important design choice is the organization's mission, which in turn helps define guiding principles, which in turn shape strategies to achieve the organization's goals and objectives. To achieve the goals and objectives, the IT organization employs resources (application systems, infrastructure, and people) and processes within a chosen organizational structure. Now we briefly consider each of these elements and then offer guidelines for considering these within an IT organizational context. (The *Design Choice Guidelines* are collected into one table in Part V.)

The Organization's Mission

The organization's *mission* identifies and articulates its primary reason for being and its distinctive competence. A good mission statement is succinct, simple, energizing, and easily remembered. It is important to articulate a mission statement and review it on a regular basis for several reasons. First, by taking the time to articulate the mission statement, the organization's senior management team has an opportunity to become better aligned and to gain a clearer understanding of what their energies should be focused toward. Second, the mission statement also provides a vehicle for communicating to employees the essence of the organization and why it exists.

Finally, the mission statement, once understood and shared, provides direction and context for other important design choices.

It helps frame answers to important questions: What specific goals and objectives ensure that our mission is accomplished? What commitments are required to accomplish our mission? Does our company culture resonate with and reinforce our mission? Are our resources focused in ways consistent with our mission? What company activities seem unrelated to our mission? And of course a host of other questions could be included as well. The point is that important long-term questions should always be considered within the context of the organization's mission.

Table 3.1: Guidelines for deciding an IT organization's Mission.

Design Decisions	Guidelines
Organization's Mission	

Identify and articulate the primary reason the IT organization exists as well as its distinctive competency. Long-term decisions should be considered in the context of the organization's mission.	To make this decision, an IT organization must determine:
	
	• What type of organization is it?
	   • An IT business within the distinct IT industry
	   • A business within a business, i.e., an IT organization within a company in another industry
	• What is the primary focus of the organization?
	   • The creating, maintaining, executing and/or hosting of self-created systems
	   • The selecting, installing, executing and/or hosting of vendor supplied systems
	   • Some combination of the two

Guiding Principles

The organization's mission statement defines the organization's reason for being, but it is not actionable in that it does not identify the ways and means of accomplishment. Basic to these ways and means are the principles that guide an organization's decisions and lay the groundwork for its culture. These principles should capture the fundamental concepts and beliefs that drive the behaviors and feelings of those who work in the organization.

These principles should also help the organization focus on acquiring people with attributes that are consistent with these behaviors and feelings. These people enable the organization to accomplish its mission and desired outcomes. The guiding principles form the core belief system that helps define the organization's culture, and hence it is important for employees to understand these principles in order to optimize their performance within that culture.

Table 3.2: Guidelines for articulating an IT
organization's Guiding Principles.

Design Decisions	Guidelines
Guiding Principles	
Identify fundamental concepts and beliefs that drive the behaviors and feelings of those who work in an IT organization, who will ultimately make decisions (choices) concerning the ways and means the IT organization achieves its mission.	The fundamental concepts and basic beliefs: • Are used to find people who share these beliefs and principles • Are the basis for decision making rather than a set of rigid, narrow rules or policies More specifically, these principles should address basic beliefs about things such as: • Technology • Dealing with others • The organization's people • Effective communication • Effective leadership • Effective management • Values

Perhaps most importantly, guiding principles, rather than a set of rigid and narrow rules or policies, should be the basis for decision making in the organization. Good decision making requires that the uniqueness of each decision be recognized, while keeping in mind that decisions need to be made within a consistent well-defined framework. The organization's guiding principles help define this framework yet can be applied with enough flexibility to take into account factors or situations that may be involved.

Strategies to Influence the External Environment

Of course strategy is an important component of any organization's success. It is through strategy that companies create sustainable competitive advantages. As Michael Porter has pointed out, this is typically accomplished by choosing strategies that allow the company to do different activities than its competitors or to do the same activities differently in order to create value. Strategies should be determined with the external environment in mind. Strategies, in fact, are often chosen to influence that environment in some way. For example, strategies are chosen to differentiate a company from its competitors, to implement or adapt best practices for efficiencies and effectiveness, to accommodate and perhaps modify regulatory constraints, and in the end to produce outcomes that provide value to clients and thus sustain the organization. [13]

We have identified two broad categories within the external environment component of the IT-OSD model: the client business environment and the IT industry environment. Table 3.3 gives guidelines for creating strategies to influence the client business environment. Two primary strategies are suggested. The first such strategy is to create strategic client partnerships, which are discussed in chapter 4. The second strategy is to educate clients about several important issues related to the *IT Value Challenge,* which is to create the proper balance of cost and quality for our clients. While a value challenge exists for all industries, this challenge can be particularly daunting for the IT industry. We take up this subject in chapters 6 and 7.

Table 3.3: *Guidelines for Strategies to Influence the Client Business Environment.*

Design Decisions	Guidelines
Strategies to Influence External Environment **Client Business Environment**	

Acquire knowledge of the client's short- and long-range business plans, financial plans, organizational structures, and current business practices and operations to gain a deeper understanding of the business intelligence necessary for creating solutions to enable success for your client.
 	
Understand regulations, laws, and governmental entities affecting your clients and accommodate and perhaps modify regulatory constraints.
 	
Acknowledge the *IT Value Challenge*, which manifests itself in an understanding gap between the client's intuitive-based perceptions and the non-intuitive-based inescapable peculiar realities of software and the software development process.
	Create strategic client partnerships by:
	• Pursuing IT *solutions* and not just *products*
	• Effectively focusing IT organization resources on client needs and priorities
	• Recognizing that the high value a client places on the quality of the interactions with their product and service suppliers is the differentiator in deciding between suppliers with similar offerings
	• Implementing a *Client-Centric Strategy* based on:
	  • The principle of *client focus*
	  • Your system architecture
	
	See chapters 4 and 5 for more details
	
	First, address the IT Value Challenge through educating the IT clients about:
	
	• The client's personal but flawed experience of software and software development because there is nothing tangible for clients to "see" to give them the intuition, experience, or knowledge they need to fully appreciate the nature of software and the software development process

	• IT value measurement based on the extent requirements and expectations have been satisfied, as jointly agreed to from the beginning of an IT work effort by the client and the organization
	• IT solution value, which involves the proper balance between effectiveness and efficiency
	
	See chapter 6 for more details
	
	Second, address the IT Value Challenge by focusing on IT as a business both strategically and tactically.
	• Strategic Focus
	   • The Hedgehog Concept
	• Tactical Focus
	   • Project management
	   • Requirements management
	   • Efficient and effective management of resources
	
	See chapter 7 for more details

Table 3.4 gives guidelines for creating strategies to influence the IT industry component of the external environment. Strategies are suggested to monitor competitors and the specific products and services that are likely to appeal to the IT organization's clients, track the availability of IT staffing in the marketplace, and implement or adapt IT industry best practices for efficiencies and effectiveness. (More details can be found in chapters 9 and 10.)

Table 3.4: Guidelines for Strategies to Influence the IT Industry Environment.

Design Decisions	Guidelines
Strategies to Influence External Environment **IT Industry Environment**	
Major components of the IT industry include competitors, the IT marketplace which supplies a workforce, technology, and industry best practices. The successful IT organization must constantly monitor the industry and craft strategies to deal with changes and realities that emerge in that environment.	Carefully monitor competitors and specific products and services that are likely to appeal to clients. Ways to gain knowledge of technology providers are to: • Schedule meetings, conference calls, on-site visits, formal training sessions, and trade show attendance to keep abreast of technology trends • Review with a technology provider upcoming activities associated with their technology • Perform technical interviews and analysis with a technology provider to determine the road map or life cycle associated with its technology Implement or adapt IT industry best practices for efficiencies and effectiveness. Gain relevant knowledge of best practices by: • Monitoring leading professional organizations, associations, and consortia that articulate and publicize frameworks in computer systems development/maintenance, operations, and management (e.g., ITIL, CMMI, PMI) • Cross-referencing these frameworks to your own set of processes in order to identify gaps and areas for possible improvement

	See chapter 9 for more details Carefully track the definition and availability of IT staffing within the marketplace by: • Conducting compensation studies to determine IT skills categorization by IT jobs and salary ranges within the marketplace • Cross-referencing these IT industry jobs to specific levels of specialization of "roles" required by the organization to accomplish its mission *See chapter 10 for more details*

Goals and Objectives

Goals and objectives are the guiding and tangible milestones by which strategies, and thus missions, are accomplished. They should be specific enough to energize work and give meaning to strategies, and they should be measurable enough that the organization's success can be evaluated unambiguously. In other words, goals and objectives are directly related to the mission as they lay out in specific and measurable terms what must be accomplished for the mission to be realized. Strategies are devised partially to achieve known goals and objectives, and more generally to provide the basic guidance for achieving new goals and objectives as they arise.

Table 3.5: Guidelines for establishing Goals and Objectives.

Design Decisions	Guidelines
Goals and Objectives	

Determining goals and objectives involves identifying guiding and tangible milestones by which strategies are accomplished. These milestones should be specific enough to energize work and give meaning to strategies, and measurable enough that success can be established unambiguously.	Each goal and objective should be chosen to advance one or more of the organization's strategies. Thus, goals and objectives should be unique to a given IT organization and its overall mission and subsequent strategies, but to aid in their articulation. Following is an example of such a goal and its measurements:
	
	Goal: To attract, select, and retain outstanding professionals and provide them with the career opportunities they seek.
	
	Measurements:
	   • Job offer decline rate
	   • One-year turnover rate
	   • Annual forced turnover rate
	   • Employee progression statistics

IT Resources

Every IT organization faces the challenge of acquiring and maintaining the following three basic types of resources.

- *Application Systems*: A group of interacting, interrelated, or interdependent computer programs designed for a specific business task or use. This is the face of the organization to the customer.

- *Infrastructure*: The underlying base or foundation (i.e., computing platforms, networks, operating systems, enabling software) required to implement and operate application systems.

- *People*: A group of skilled IT personnel to build and maintain the application systems and the infrastructure.

To meet the challenge of managing its infrastructure and application systems resources, an IT organization should complete the identification, development, and use of a *system architecture* consistent with and supportive of its overall mission. The system architecture is the central element in determining the organization's capabilities, and it is these capabilities that the processes and organizational structure attempt to mobilize. Using the system architecture as a guide, organizational units can be identified and assigned responsibility to efficiently acquire and maintain all or some portion of the infrastructure and the application systems resources. Each organizational unit can then be identified as responsible for, or a participant in, all or some portion of the highly defined, repeatable processes required to support the IT resources for which it is responsible. Using the architecture as a guide in this design ensures that the processes and organizational structure are arranged around and connected with organizational capabilities, and thus results in these being better positioned to serve client needs and requests.

To meet the challenge of managing its people resource, an IT organization must complete the identification of *IT roles*. These roles must be successfully fulfilled as they relate to the IT organization's framework of administrative and operational processes. Hence the organizational structure must also provide for the acquisition, development, and general "care and feeding" of the people filling these roles.

Table 3.6: Guidelines for Managing Resources.

Design Decisions	Guidelines
Managing IT Resources	
We have identified three basic types of IT resources. • *Application Systems:* A group of interacting, interrelated, or interdependent computer programs designed for a specific business task or use. This is the face of the organization to customer. • *Infrastructure:* The underlying base or foundation (i.e., computing platforms, networks, operating systems, enabling software) required to implement and operate application systems. • *People:* A group of skilled IT personnel to build and maintain the application systems and the infrastructure.	To meet the challenge of managing its infrastructure and application systems resources, an IT organization should complete the identification, development, and use of a system architecture consistent with and supportive of its overall mission. *See chapter 5 for more details* To meet the challenge of managing its people resource, an IT organization must: • Provide for the acquisition, development, and general "care and feeding" of the people • Define a set of IT roles commensurate with the organization's framework of administrative and operational processes • Manage people within these roles so that they are successfully fulfilled in order to achieve the organization's mission *See chapter 10 for more details*

IT Processes

A second challenge for any IT organization concerns process, which is defined as a series of actions or operations that bring about a predictable result or outcome. The challenge is to correctly identify and implement a highly integrated, repeatable, and scalable set of administrative and operational processes that the organization must perform to be successful. An important strategy to be used to fulfill this challenge is the adaptation of selected IT industry best-practice frameworks, where appropriate, for various elements of an IT organization's administration and operations.

Table 3.7: Guidelines for Implementing Processes.

Design Decisions	Guidelines
Implement Processes	

The successful IT organization must correctly identify and implement a highly integrated, repeatable, scalable, and complete set of administrative and operational processes that the organization can utilize to produce the required outcomes to meet its mission.	Using a process of adaptation from selected IT industry best-practice frameworks along with experience, we have articulated what we believe to be a *complete* IT process framework, applicable to any IT organization, comprising the following nine fundamental processes distributed among three major process groups:
	
	 Adaptive Change
	    1. Adaptive Change Management
	
	 Business Perspective
	    2. Line of Business (LOB) management
	    3. Client Management
	
	 System Factory
	    4. System Architecture Management
	    5. Application Systems Management
	    6. Service Management
	    7. Information and Communication Technology (ICT) Infrastructure Management
	    8. Security and Audit Management
	    9. Enabling Support Management
	
	 See chapter 9 for more details

Organizational Structure

An additional and related challenge concerns organizational structure. By organizational structure, we mean the formal decision-making framework by which tasks within an organization are divided, grouped, coordinated, and implemented. The challenge is to design an organizational structure that interconnects and aligns the organization's resources and processes for the proper use of chosen organizational strategies that ensure realization of the organization's mission. The choice of the appropriate processes and an organizational structure to properly connect them to IT resources is a complex issue and should be approached in a systematic way. The following considerations provide a rational approach to resolving this issue. (We explore these ideas in Part III.)

Table 3.8: *Guidelines for deciding Organizational Structure.*

Design Decisions	Guidelines
Organizational Structure	
To produce its desired outcomes, the IT organization must identify and implement an organizational structure that interconnects and aligns the organization's resources and processes.	An organizational structure called the *Hierarchical Matrix* structure offers some unique advantages to an IT organization. This structure: • Blends some of the most desirable features of the functional and strong matrix organizational structure approaches • Is particularly relevant to the challenge of balancing efficiency and effectiveness • Provides the IT organization the capabilities to operate with scarce resources, while maintaining technical expertise and the flexibility to deliver excellent products and services **See chapter 8 for more details**

Organizational Culture and Outcomes

Organizational culture is the collective embodiment of the predominating attitudes and behavior that characterize the functioning of an organization. Culture is the organizational philosophy (as articulated in the mission, guiding principles, and strategies) in action. Another way to view organizational culture is that it captures "how things are done around here," meaning that it is a system of formal and informal rules that spell out how people are to behave most of the time. In essence, culture is the intangible "personality of the organization." As such, it can be thought of as the synthesis of values, myths, heroes, and symbols that have assumed important meaning to the people who work in a given organization.

Culture is formed and changes slowly over long periods of time. Attempting to implement changes that are counter to organizational culture can be daunting and often unsuccessful. Similarly, the successful implementation of changes designed to modify the culture require great effort, skill, and patience. A "bad" culture can be a barrier to the organization's success, just as a "good" culture can be one of the organization's strengths and competitive advantages.

It is worth noting that benefits are not culture. The benefits that an organization offers to its staff are often confused with culture, but they do not define culture. Benefits can change, sometimes quickly, based on the business environment; culture, as we have noted, has great inertia. Good benefits can be important to attracting and hiring good people, but assuming benefits are kept at adequate levels, they are less important in the long run for retaining those people. More important is the energy and enthusiasm people derive from the organization's culture.

Outcomes are those end results that define the organization's success. These are generally articulated based on a combination of the organization's capabilities and its clients' expectations. It is important to make sure that the outcomes are well-defined and specific enough to be measurable. If outcomes are ambiguously phrased or poorly constructed, attempts to measure them can be flawed or perhaps futile. Without meaningful measurement, the organization has no firm basis on which to assess its success. This doesn't mean that every outcome must be inherently quantitative, but some meaningful quantitative or qualitative measure of the achievement of the outcome must be possible and accessible.

Adaptive Change and the IT-OSD Model

As we have discussed, the IT-OSD model is intended as a framework that an IT organization can use to guide an evolutionary and systematic approach to adaptive change. To function effectively as such a framework, the model itself must be flexible and adaptive enough to evolve. Overseeing such adaptation and evolution is the job of the management and leadership teams of the organization.

In this context, we define *leadership* as a set of activities that help direct, align, and inspire actions on the part of large numbers of people to organize in the first place and adapt for success in significantly changing circumstances. On the other hand, *management* focuses on activities that produce a degree of predictability and order through a set of processes that can keep a complicated system of resources (people and technology) running smoothly.

As a consequence of these definitions, the culture and vision necessary to create and maintain the organization's mission, guiding principles, and strategies tend to be the province of leadership. Overseeing structure and processes and the outcomes these produce tend to be the province of management. Figure 3.2 illustrates the complementary nature of leadership and management. (Chapter 12 explores these ideas further.)

Application of the Model

The I/S Division of BlueCross BlueShield of South Carolina has used the IT-OSD model as a framework to guide its evolutionary and systematic approach to adaptive change since 2004. A few applications of the model have proved particularly advantageous:

- The significant role that the external influence of IT industry best practices has played in shaping the definition of the fundamental processes the division uses, its view of IT service and its management, and the integration of the application system development methodology and the infrastructure development and deployment methodology.

- The external influence of IT industry definitions of skill sets and specialties in shaping the division's roles.

- The division's proactive approach to organizational learning as a strategy to enable adaptive change and to influence deficiencies in the kinds of skill sets being supplied by educational providers supporting the industry.

- The articulation of a comprehensive set of guiding principles governing the areas of people, technology, and management practices.

- The importance of the system architecture in organizing people and infrastructure for optimum outcomes.

- The importance of understanding the client business environment and using it as a competitive advantage.

- The increased ability to explain and communicate organizational culture, strategies, and vision.

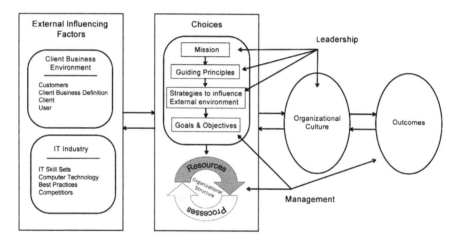

Figure 3.2: *Overseeing the evolution of an IT-OSD model for an organization.*

Part II
Enabling Client Value

Chapter 4

Strategic Client Partnerships: Implementing a Client-Centric Strategy

Never treat your audience as customers, always as partners.

Jimmy Stewart

Successful organizations value the client relationships they have, and they spend considerable time and effort to develop and nurture these relationships. Although these relationships can help the organization reap many benefits, among the most important of these are the strategic advantages that are possible with trusted client partners. Creating such relationships requires careful planning and a deliberate strategy. Long-term client loyalty and trust requires a long-term commitment. This begins by identifying clients who believe in the organization's products and services and who recognize the value the organization delivers. These are the clients who are most likely to understand and appreciate the organization's expertise and capabilities. When these clients are themselves innovators and change leaders in their field, the stage is set for the development of *strategic partnerships*. These partnerships can provide tremendous mutual benefits for the client and the organization.

For IT organizations, a primary strategic benefit that can be derived from strategic partnerships is a deeper understanding of the business intelligence necessary for creating innovative solutions that enable success within the client's business environment. As we saw in chapter 2, business intelligence is critical for directing and enhancing the evolutionary system development approach, a key factor for an IT organization's ultimate success. In fact, Ranjay Gulati asserts that the ability to "listen carefully to create relevancy for customers may be a more important business value than innovation." [14] And even in industries being challenged by the commoditization of services and products, Mark Vandenbosch and Niraj Dawar found that "some companies have figured out how to outdistance rivals through customer-focused strategies that are virtually imitation-proof." [15]

The client organization in such a strategic partnership derives the benefit of IT systems that integrate the advantages of technical *and* business innovations. Importantly, such systems can enhance the client's competitive advantages, since client-tailored systems have the potential to help the client achieve true differentiation from its competitors. In addition, if these systems have been developed within a partnership with the IT organization, they are often difficult to duplicate or emulate, and are therefore all the more strategically valuable.

Products versus Solutions

It is common for service and product providers to proclaim that they are in the business of providing "solutions" for their clients. However, all too often companies view a client's problems—and the solutions they provide for these—only through the lens of their own existing products and services. Indeed, it can be difficult to make the transition from the product/service view to a true solutions view. Doing this means seeing the world from the client's perspective and therefore understanding the true nature of the challenges and opportunities that the client faces.

In order for solutions to provide clients the competitive advantages they seek, these solutions must satisfy three requirements.

First, they must address problems that are truly meaningful to the client. That is, the problems they solve and the processes they support must be within the competitive or competitive-enabling work that the client performs to differentiate its outcomes from those of its competitors. Second, the solutions themselves must provide real value, meaning that they must achieve significant outcomes at a high level of quality within acceptable cost parameters. And third, to provide a sustainable competitive advantage, the solutions must be difficult for the client's competitors to replicate.

The understanding of the client business environment inherent in the IT-OSD model can facilitate all three of these requirements. The IT-OSD model provides the framework for developing a strategic relationship between an IT organization and a client. It highlights for the IT organization the context of such a relationship, namely the client business environment as a major external influence. In addition, as we explore in the next chapter, a system architecture tailored to meet strategic clients' core needs can form the technical foundation for building the capabilities that enable successful strategic client relationships.

If the IT organization can achieve the significant understanding of the client business environment suggested by these considerations, then the organization is focused on problems that are meaningful to the client. In other words, the IT organization and the client engaged in a strategic partnership are able to reach agreement on *the right problems* to work on. In addition, the solutions supplied to the client by leveraging the system architecture are capable of delivering high value to the client provided the system architecture has been organized for this purpose. So delivering *the right solutions*—that is, solutions with true value—can be achieved. And finally, if solutions are delivered via application systems that were developed using the evolutionary approach discussed in chapter 2, the very hallmark of this approach is that it supports the parallel evolution of business intelligence and technological innovation. As a consequence, the resulting solutions are difficult for the client's competitors to replicate.

Elevating the Importance of Client Interactions

Few would argue with the idea that understanding a client's needs, aspirations, and opportunities would permit any organization to provide better products and services for that client. But recognizing the value of productive client interactions and achieving this are not the same. How does an organization develop and cultivate the appropriate interactions?

In a five-year study, Gulati found that many companies, while anxious to offer clients solutions, simply aren't set up to deliver them without significant changes in organizational structure and processes. More specifically, he found that often the organization's expertise and knowledge are housed in internal silos that make it difficult to effectively focus resources on client needs and priorities. However, in the study he did find some organizations that had been successful in their efforts to deliver solutions that offered true value to their clients. He further identified the four categories of activities common to these organizations that seemed to play key roles in this success:

- Coordination for client focus

- Cooperation as a basic element of culture

- Capability building

- Connections with external partners

He labeled these four categories the *four C's of customer focus*, and they are particularly relevant for an IT organization's development of strategic partnerships.

Coordination involves the sharing of client-related information and decision making across internal organizational boundaries. Knowledge about the client and its business environment should be freely shared within the IT organization, and decisions concerning the client should be made with full access to this information and the judgments and opinions of all those in the organization who interact with the client. This involves establishing structural mechanisms and processes that allow employees to improve their focus on the client by facilitating activities and the flow of information across units. If this is done, though the organization may have different internal groups who interact with a client, it can present a coordinated, united front to the client. Such an approach enables the organization to better understand the client's business and at the same time raise the client's level of confidence in the organization's commitment to it.

To accomplish the desired level of coordination with respect to its clients, an organization must encourage a culture of *cooperation* across internal boundaries. In other words, the organization should encourage those in all parts of the organization to work together in the interest of identifying and meeting client needs. An important activity toward this end is to formulate and make clear the organization's expectations of employee behaviors that produce effective internal knowledge sharing about clients. To ensure that such behavioral objectives are met, the organization should devise appropriate metrics to assess performance relative to these objectives and institute a reward system that reinforces their value.

Setting and reinforcing the coordination of the organization's client activities as an organizational objective is an essential component of a client-centric strategy. However, to ensure the success of such a strategy, the organization must also build the *capabilities* necessary for the implementation of the strategy. This requires ensuring that enough people in the organization have the skills to oversee the delivery of effective and valued client solutions as well as defining a clear career path for employees with those skills.

There are three such capabilities that are directly applicable to an IT organization. First the organization must develop employees who have a deep knowledge of each client and their business environment. Such knowledge will be a prerequisite to understanding the client's present needs and anticipating possible future needs. Second, persons with knowledge and experience with the organization's multiple products and services must be developed and supported, and ready access across the organization to this knowledge and experience must be assured. If the organization is to supply solutions of value to clients, it must have those who can identify—and "assemble" if necessary—those solutions. And finally, the organization must develop persons with the capability and perspective to transcend internal boundaries for the purpose of aligning organizational resources and expertise to address client needs once they are identified.

Building *connections* with external partners so that others' expertise and cost-effectiveness can be leveraged when possible is also important to ensuring the value that clients expect. These partners may be vendors, subsidiaries, or even other clients. The point is that the IT organization should leverage its expertise in its own field and the set of relationships inherent in its position in the IT industry for the benefit of its clients. These connections can be optimized for client value only when the coordination, cooperation, and capabilities already described are in place within the IT organization.

What Do Clients Value?

In today's marketplace it has become increasingly challenging for organizations to differentiate themselves through product lines alone. Open standards, the free flow of information, and the global availability of talent make it difficult to create and sustain competitive advantages. Vandenbosch and Dawar put it this way:

> Talk to the senior executives of any progressive company today and they will tell you about its huge investments in innovation, bulging new-product pipelines, proprietary technologies, and relentless drive to shrink time to market. They'll also admit that these efforts have not helped them outrun the competition. Although businesses are moving faster than ever, competitors are constantly nipping at their heels, emulating new products, replicating entire product-development systems and processes, and keeping pace on the same treadmill. New products may generate hefty returns, but the advantage is short-lived. These days, a company's rivals are likely to be world-class sprinters.

While these observations hold true in many industries, they are especially applicable to the IT industry.

These considerations led Vandenbosch and Dawar to conduct a three-year study collecting data from over 1,500 senior executives, in an attempt to answer the following question. What criteria *beyond product* do customers turn to when making decisions to buy from one company over another? The most common answer was that customers seem to place a high value on the *quality of their interactions* with their suppliers. They cited such factors as convenience, cost containment, trust and confidence leading to reduced risks, and strength of relationship as important. Several strategies common to those organizations that had been successful at creating these kinds of relationships emerged from the study. Increased opportunities to contain costs and limit risks are central features for each of these strategies. When the common cost and schedule overruns characteristic of the IT industry are considered, these strategies take on even more relevance for an IT organization.

The first strategy involves *leveraging economies of scope* inherent in serving multiple clients. This is enabled by recognizing needs, common or similar across multiple clients, that the organization either has, or can build, the capability of satisfying. Clients then have the opportunity to realize cost savings through the IT organization's abilities to leverage the development and support costs of a product or service across several clients. At the same time, the IT organization may be willing to assume a substantial portion of the risk of developing new functions or enhancing existing ones with the promise of the increased returns on the effort made possible by offering these to multiple clients. Clearly, the organizations that are best able to take advantage of these economies of scope are the ones that have adopted the practices of coordination and cooperation relative to client focus that we discussed earlier. If employees are encouraged to approach all client requests and issues from an economy-of-scope perspective and share their observations across internal boundaries, the organization is in a far better position to recognize and act on the potential for creating economies of scope that benefit not only the IT organization but its clients as well.

A second strategy focuses on listening closely to clients to *understand gaps and deficiencies in current products and services*—supplied by the IT organization or a competitor—with the aim of identifying promising new product or product enhancement opportunities. There are multiple benefits the IT organization can offer its clients through this strategy. For example, the organization may be able to leverage existing products and services to meet new and changing requirements, reducing both the cost and risk to the client in satisfying the given need. If new product development is called for that more squarely fits the organization's capabilities than it does the client's capabilities and expertise, once again the client's risks may be substantially reduced over those associated with their own development of the capability. This approach not only simplifies the given client's route to the benefits of the new product but also offers the organization additional opportunities to leverage the development effort with other clients who may have similar needs. It also opens the door for innovations with other clients who may not have yet recognized these needs.

Even if the IT organization does not have the internal capabilities to completely satisfy the identified needs, there may be opportunities to leverage its expertise to act as a broker or synthesizer to identify relevant industry standards and bring key complementors into a partnership to create the appropriate solutions. Once again, the client benefits from the reduced risks made possible by working through the same trusted source to obtain the needed solution. The client may also benefit from the lower search and evaluation costs that can come from this approach. In other words, the IT organization supplies a key advantage to the client by leveraging its expertise in both the client business area and in its own solutions provider network.

When strategic client partnerships are developed, opportunities may also arise for shared business activities. The IT organization may be able to coordinate or combine activities with the customer to lower the client's operating and transaction costs. An example could be hosting selected application systems for the client. A hosting solution might significantly reduce the client's costs of supplying infrastructure and service support for the system as well as reduce both the cost and time for modifying the system's functionalities and performance. In addition, the IT organization's development and design expertise could also ensure longer effective lifetimes for such systems and thus offer enhanced protection of the client's investment.

Enabling Client Focus

We have identified some of the mutual advantages that the IT organization and its clients can realize by building close client relationships. In this section we explore the optimal dynamic between the organization and the client in a strategic partnership. Can we define the roles that the client and the IT organization each assume to ensure that both reap the optimal benefits from the partnership? In all walks of life, the most productive relationships recognize the strengths and weaknesses of each partner, then organize the dynamics of the relationship to minimize the partnership's collective weaknesses and maximize its collective strengths. We believe the way to accomplish this for an IT organization and its strategic clients is through what we call the principle of *client focus.*

Client focus is built around a common-sense division of labor principle. The ideal IT organization-client relationships allows the client to focus on what it knows best—succeeding in its business environment. By the same reasoning, the IT organization should be allowed to focus on its expertise in providing outstanding solutions that are appropriate and cost-effective for the client's business needs.

The client focus principle succeeds when there is a high degree of mutual trust in the relationship. The client must trust the IT organization to deliver value by developing systems of high quality for reasonable costs. Conversely, the organization must be able to trust the client to share its business expertise so that the systems being built fully integrate innovative technology *and* innovative business intelligence and thus provide the long-term value that makes both successful. Distrust on either side makes the target value proposition difficult, if not impossible, to achieve.

The risks in such a partnership must also be recognized, acknowledged, and dealt with by both the IT organization and the client. The client does not want to be put in the position of feeling that it is held hostage by the IT organization. Hence, the organization must operate with integrity in delivering honest value to the client and not exploit or take undue advantage of potential lock-in strategies that it could employ. Neither should it build in artificial or exorbitant switching costs for the client, should the client wish to consider other suppliers.

On the other hand, the client must freely share essential business information and strategies with the IT organization and make a reasonable commitment to a long-term relationship. The dangers for the IT organization are that it could expend tremendous effort to build systems tailored for a client, only to find that the client shifts suppliers before the organization's return on this investment can be realized, or that the business knowledge shared by the client did not have long-term value. Further, if the IT organization expects to leverage the systems being built with other clients based on economies of scope—and this is a likely and desirable objective—then there must be clear nondisclosure understandings about the amount of embedded client-specific business knowledge involved in this process.

If trust can be built, the client-focus approach pays excellent dividends. This approach allows the client organization to focus on its business problems, challenges, and opportunities, while the IT organization focuses on helping the client understand the possibilities and promise that IT solutions could enhance the client's responses to these challenges. Most importantly, this strategic relationship enables the kind of organic growth of information systems that embed both technical and business excellence—exactly the kinds of systems that can fuel competitive advantages for both the client and the IT organization. This kind of growth reduces development costs and risks for both client and IT organizations. The client avoids the cost and risk of getting solutions from an IT organization that does not possess sufficient knowledge about its business environment. On the other hand, the IT organization minimizes the risk of wasted resources expended in developing solutions that prove to be insufficient to meet the business challenges for which they were intended.

Implementing a Client-Centric Strategy: An Example

The particular organizational setting in which the BlueCross BlueShield of South Carolina I/S Division operates has shaped the kinds of strategic client relationships the division has developed. The parent company is organized as a holding company for a group of relatively independent line-of-business (LOB) oriented insurance-related companies. Each of these LOB companies operates as a separate entity with the exception of two functions: financial reporting and information technology. Both the financial reporting system and the information technology systems are centralized, and these two entities report directly to the parent company CEO. Some of the LOBs compete in the same insurance markets, with the guiding restriction that they are allowed to compete with their sibling LOBs based on products and services but not based on price.

While not operated directly as a profit center, the I/S Division is nonetheless a relatively independent "company within a company," offering IT products and services to the various LOBs. These services are contracted for and paid for by the management teams of the various LOBs, and while the division is the supplier of preference for the LOBs, the LOBs do have the option of seeking IT services and products from other sources through a defined approval process.

Therefore, the division has the opportunity to develop close strategic partnerships with these clients, although the partnerships are still set in the context of paying clients who have their own distinct business environments. In other words, while being a "supplier of preference" for these clients offers the division opportunities to develop strategically important relationships, these relationships are still governed by the same underlying realities and constraints implicit and inherent for any supplier/client relationship.

Over the past several decades, the division has indeed developed and nurtured strong, mutually beneficial strategic partnerships with a number of these clients. For each business represented by these clients and in many cases for substructures within the business, the customers, client business definition, clients, and users are identified to provide the specific business requirements of a given client environment to be supported.

These client relationships have been enhanced by the adoption of guiding principles that spell out the underlying philosophy and expectations that help define a client-centric culture within the division. This culture is built on the philosophy of *client focus*, discussed earlier, which stresses the importance of allowing each client to focus on its own core-business competencies, while the division focuses on world-class delivery of the products and services to meet each client's needs. This philosophy sets the context for the development of systems that combine the best available business knowledge with innovative and highly leveraged technical solutions. It is this combination that has provided significant strategic partnership payoffs for both the division and its clients.

In addition, the management of client relationships has been elevated to a specialty within the organization, and this specialty is nurtured by a well-defined client management organization within the overall I/S organization. The client management organization within the I/S Division employs processes to establish and maintain relationships and ensure appropriate client communication, client focus, and client control of priorities by coordinating with clients at strategic, tactical, and operational levels. The client management unit is a *service organization*, meaning that it is not directly accountable for product lines, but rather focuses on providing a specific set of services for the client.

Two important pillars lay the foundation for the client-centric strategy that the I/S Division has embraced. As we discussed in chapter 3, the IT-OSD model, with its emphasis on the importance of the client business environment as one of the central external influences on any IT organization, encourages the division to gain an excellent understanding of the client business and the core competencies that enable the organization's clients to be successful. The model also provides a reminder and a framework to constantly scan that portion of the external environment as an important source of potential changes that the organization may need to adapt to. The second pillar, the division's system architecture, supplies the capability to optimize the benefits of a client-centric strategy.

In summary, it is fair to say that it would be difficult to overestimate the importance of strategic client partnerships to the remarkable success that the BlueCross BlueShield of SC I/S Division has enjoyed over the past two decades. These partnerships have offered the division the opportunity to employ an organic evolutionary process to develop and leverage a highly integrated system architecture that has provided a tremendous flywheel for sustaining the organization's growth. One of the fundamental strengths of this architecture is its intricate combination of technological innovation and the deep business intelligence gained from the insurance industry largely through strategic client partnerships. Indeed, it is this combination that has created the competitive advantage that the architecture flywheel embodies—a competitive advantage that has proved both sustainable and difficult to emulate.

Chapter 5

System Architecture: Foundation for the Value of IT

"Think Simple" as my old master used to say—meaning reduce the whole of its parts into the simplest terms, getting back to first principles.

Frank Lloyd Wright

The strategic value of IT is realized by the extent to which IT systems enable clients to meet their current business objectives and successfully exploit emerging business opportunities. IT resources must be managed to meet these business objectives efficiently and effectively. Clients expect the timely delivery of reliable, innovative systems at a reasonable cost. They have expectations that all newly delivered components will work smoothly with existing systems, exchanging information with these systems in a natural and even transparent way. And they expect a minimum of disruption to their work flow as they incorporate the new components. These expectations translate into daunting challenges for the software development organization, yet the success of the organization depends on the realization of this value proposition. As we will see, a well-designed system architecture is an essential foundation for this realization.

System Architecture Defined

To consistently meet the challenge of efficiently and effectively managing its resources, it is essential for an IT organization to identify and develop a well-designed and well-understood system architecture. Note that our definition of *IT organization* includes stand-alone IT companies or IT organizational units within larger companies that are responsible for the delivery of IT products and services. There are varying interpretations of what a system architecture is. Before we discuss why a well-designed system architecture is so important, we begin by first defining what we mean by this term.

Most definitions of the term *architecture* reflect the idea of over-all structure or organization. For example, IEEE Standard 610 defines architecture as "the organizing structure of a system." [16] David Garlan and Dewayne Perry define software architecture as "the structure of the components of a program/system, their interrelationships, and principles and guidelines governing their design and evolution over time." [17] And finally, the Merriam-Webster's Collegiate Dictionary defines the term *architectural* as "having, or conceived of as having, a single unified design, form, or structure." [18]

Our definition of *system architecture* is consistent with these ideas, but also includes an important additional element:

> A system architecture defines the capabilities required to produce IT products and services that meet clients' business needs, describes how these products and services are to be organized and provided, specifies what IT resources they require, and identifies what common product and service components can be leveraged across the needs of multiple clients.

The additional element is the inherent and essential connection between the system architecture and clients' business needs. To establish this connection, the IT organization must understand the client business structure, what information is being exchanged between the client and other business entities in support of the client's business, and what business systems are required by the client's business to support the information exchange. This connection is often misunderstood, inadequately considered, or even overlooked completely in decision making about IT system architecture. Alexander Drobik, vice president of Gartner Research, describes it as follows: "[To the IT people] enterprise architecture refers to how IT components fit together, just as [to the business people] a business architecture describes how the business is put together. In reality, they are the opposite sides of the same coin—joined completely." [19] Another way to phrase this is to observe that a system architecture is designed to enable the successful translation of business strategy into technical strategy. Indeed, it is exactly this inseparable connection that should be reflected in the organization and structure of the architecture and is built into our definition of a system architecture.

System architecture as we define it is in place to provide an active approach to developing and maintaining the strategic agility needed to address effectively the IT organization's various clients' needs and business opportunities. Without a well-understood and maintained architecture providing guidance to system analysts, developers, and programmers, business requirements cannot be met in an efficient and effective manner. It is important to note that this is not a matter of an IT organization choosing whether it does or does not *have* a system architecture. Every organization has one. The issue is rather whether the organization invests the effort to articulate and understand its architecture and take an active approach to developing and maintaining it.

Software and Complexity

To better understand the use of a system architecture by an IT organization, it is instructive to consider some of the fundamental characteristics of *software*. Whether an organization's mission is the creation, maintenance, and execution of self-created systems or the selection, installation, and execution of vendor-supplied systems, at the heart of every computer system is the software that supports the specific requirements of a given client.

Over the past few decades, the complexity of software systems has increased substantially. We now routinely tackle programming problems with solutions that require the effort of thousands of person-hours to complete. Even larger programming projects are committed to as well, requiring hundreds of *person-years* to develop. And as large integrated systems are developed over years, the amount of business intelligence, the levels of logical intricacy, and the sheer effort required to build these are daunting.

More than thirty years ago, Brooks observed that the complexity inherent in large software projects does not grow linearly with the scope and purpose of the product being delivered. In his analysis, he differentiated the following types of software outcomes:

- *Program:* A program is complete in itself and written often by a single author. Such a product is ready to be *run by its author* on the system on which it was developed and for the exact purpose the author had in mind when writing it.

- *Program Product:* A program product is a program that can be *run, tested, repaired, and extended by other* professional programmers for many different sets of data. It may be based on a simple program, but it must be constructed with a certain degree of flexibility and usuability in mind. It must be well-documented so that others can fix it, modify it, and extend it as the need arises.

- *Program System:* A program system is *a collection of interacting programs usable in a single operational environment* for many sets of data that can be run, tested, repaired, and extended by other professional programmers. A program system constitutes an entire facility for processing large tasks and can be used by non-programming personnel in support of their routine tasks.

- *System Product:* A system product is *a collection of interacting programs usable in many operational environments* for many sets of data that can be run, tested, repaired, and extended by other professional programmers. A system product constitutes an entire facility for processing large tasks and is constructed with a degree of flexibility and usability that makes it usable by non-programming personnel in support of their routine tasks. It must be well-documented so that others can fix it, modify it, and extend it as the need arises. This kind of product is the goal of most large system programming efforts. [1]

Not surprisingly, the difficulties associated with producing these types of software differ dramatically. Adapting Brooks' rules of thumb, we get the approximate complexity/cost multiplier factors shown in figure 5.1 as we move from a simple program to the other types of software systems. Clearly then, it is an increasing challenge to maintain intellectual control over software complexity as we move from designing and building a program, to designing and integrating a set of programs into a robust, tested, documented, and supported system, and finally to designing and synthesizing a system into a robust, tested, documented, and supported system product.

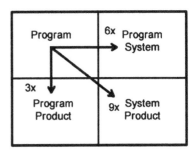

Software Outcome Types, and Estimated Cost/Complexity Multipliers

Figure 5.1: *Complexity/Cost multipliers*

The complexity Brooks described emanates from the thought process required in developing system products. Obviously, one person does not design and develop a software system product requiring hundreds of years of person-hours of effort. To compensate for this, the thought process must ensure conceptual integrity within software that is developed by teams of many people. The goal is to ensure that the underlying design emanates from, or at least that it appears to emanate from, one mind or a small group of agreeing minds. Even more difficult is to maintain this conceptual integrity over time as large system products are modified and extended by increasing numbers of programmers, most of whom had no involvement in the original design and development effort. This can be accomplished only if the thought process ensures that one mind or a small group of agreeing minds is always in control of the design and that new components are designed within an appropriately constrained structure and set of possibilities.

Finally, the thought process must ensure a conceptual integrity and consistency in what the software presents to each of its users. The software should present an accessible and understandable mental model of the application and the strategies to be employed for using the application. The tactics used in specifying actions and parameters in the user interface should be consistent and coherent. In short, users should clearly perceive the conceptual integrity of the application, which is ultimately the most important factor in its ease of use.

System Architecture and Complexity

Using a metaphor drawn from the construction industry, Grady Booch and colleagues have observed that large programming system products can take on complexity comparable to a skyscraper, with its many interconnected subsystems. Building these structures requires careful attention to the design and integration of subsystems such as the electrical network, the plumbing system, the heating and air conditioning systems, the access system (elevators, stairwells), and the sprinkler system—in addition to the basic construction tasks. [20]

Of course, we cannot use the same ad hoc approach we might use to build dog houses to build skyscrapers and retain any reasonable expectation of success. As we move from dog houses to skyscrapers, so to speak, architectural issues assume greater and greater importance. Clearly, complexity is a key concern that we would like the system architecture to address. This complexity manifests itself in two primary areas: *intellectual complexity* and *managerial complexity*.

Intellectual complexity is an inherent characteristic of the system being built, and may arise from several sources, such as the complexity of the solution to the underlying problem being addressed by the system, the scope or sheer size of the system, the novelty or innovative character of the system, the interconnectedness with and dependencies on other systems or components, or the inherent complexities of the technologies to be employed. A well-designed system architecture can make complex systems more understandable and intellectually manageable by providing abstractions that hide unnecessary detail, by employing unifying and simplifying concepts, by imposing a logical decomposition of the system, by ensuring the intellectual coherence of the various components of the system, and by ensuring only the required minimum of logical coupling between different components.

On the other hand, managerial complexity is implicit in the organization and execution of the processes employed in building the system. This complexity may arise from the scope and size of a project, the communication overhead of dealing with large numbers of workers on the project, and the interconnectedness with and dependencies on other systems or external entities. Once again, the system architecture can help reduce this complexity and make the development of the system easier to manage. It can do this by providing a natural (relative to the architecture) scheme for decomposing the work needed. The architectural view of the system not only makes the assignment of work more logically meaningful, it also gives the various components of the work itself more coherence. The big picture provided by the system architecture also helps streamline and simplify the communication lines required for the management of the work, and the clearer understanding of the various work product interfaces that the architecture can provide reduces the need for much of this communication. Finally, the system architecture provides knowledge about, and access to, reusable components that can be leveraged to reduce the amount of actual work needed to build the product.

Put another way, understanding and managing the system architecture can help an organization avoid certain undesirable and limiting outcomes. One such undesirable outcome is the haphazard evolution of a disconnected and inflexible system architecture. Remember that software developers have, if they are unconstrained, many degrees of freedom in addressing clients' problems and opportunities. If left on their own, developers often exercise remarkable creativity in designing elegant and innovative solutions that may be near optimal for the specific application at hand. The problem is that a collection of locally optimal applications (no matter how elegant and innovative these may be) is not likely to form an optimal system when bundled together. In fact, when little direction and few constraints are provided, the resulting system is typically nowhere near optimal and likely to fail in providing any systemic conceptual integrity or reusability.

In this case, maintenance becomes an expensive and error-prone nightmare. The absence of consistent approaches and common design principles make every system component potentially a functional silo that, unless it has been expertly and extensively documented, represents a complex puzzle to any programmer who was not involved in its original design. Even if appropriate documentation is there, the process of modifying numerous one-of-a-kind designs is still likely to be slow and arduous. In short, bottom-up technical design and decision making produce a tangled web of non-interoperable, difficult to maintain, logically disconnected applications. This outcome all but guarantees that the organization cannot exhibit the flexibility and adaptability required to successfully keep pace with its clients' evolving business needs and strategies.

Of course, the main purpose of a well-designed system architecture, enforced and informed by a common set of design principles and standards, is not to discourage software developer creativity. Rather, its purpose is to direct and funnel that creativity into designing innovative solutions that optimize the *overall* purpose of the architecture, which is to provide the flexibility and leveraging ability to deliver value to the organization's clients. There are always tradeoffs in decisions about technology solutions and directions. The well-designed and well-understood system architecture provides a big-picture framework within which these tradeoffs can be evaluated more wisely for the overall organization.

The well-designed system architecture also allows the organization to address issues whose scope spans organizational boundaries such as different business units or functional groups. Examples of some common concerns are: shared access to information; reduced redundancy in development leading to lower costs; and global system features such as interface and usability standards, interoperability, security, and system access methods or portals. It would be difficult if not impossible to address these issues effectively and efficiently in individual organizational units.

High Quality System Architecture Design

We have argued that one of the primary advantages of a good system architecture design is a logically coherent decomposition of the system to address both intellectual and managerial complexity. But are all logical decompositions created equal? If not, how do we decide how to break a system up into pieces? Certainly a good decomposition satisfies the principle of loose coupling between components and is characterized by clearly defined interfaces, allowing the individual components to be dealt with in relatively independent ways. But while these are necessary conditions for a good decomposition, they are not sufficient.

Remember that at the beginning of our discussion, we asserted that there should be a link between client business needs and the architecture. The structure of the system architecture must support the business functionality or services required of the system. In other words, it is the system's *business capabilities and functionalities* as expressed in the dynamic behavior of the system that should be reflected in the decomposition design of the architecture. The system architecture is an attempt to make a system of great complexity accessible. It recognizes that no one person or small group can hold complex systems "in their heads." Hence a measure of quality of the architecture's design is to evaluate the effectiveness of the way it decomposes the overall system. Focusing first on business capabilities and functionalities that support core competencies, then moving to the technical design of those capabilities, seems a good way to approach this problem.

An alternative approach that still retains the link to the supported businesses would be to focus on *business processes* rather than on capabilities. A process focus would first consider business activities to see how these produce outcomes. Some enterprise resource planning systems take this approach. When a company adopts such a system, the chances of a successful implementation depend on the degree to which the organization's processes match those modeled in the system. The system is process-oriented and works well if the interrelationships between technology, processes, skills, and culture match up well. If the match is poor, the successful implementation of such a system is a greater challenge and requires broad-based process changes within the organization.

Capabilities are not processes—a process *executes* a capability using a combination of people and technology. The focus of capability design is on outcomes and the effective use of resources to produce a differentiating capability or an essential supporting capability. The capability focus for system decomposition has several advantages over a process focus. First, different business processes might achieve the same capability, so business capability is the more fundamental entity. For example, different clients may require identical (or closely related) capabilities or functionality, yet they may employ different processes to realize the capability. Second, a system architecture organized around business capabilities is easier for clients to understand, which enables better client communications. And finally, the capability approach makes it easier for the IT organization to map architectural components to client requests for new products. This in turn allows for more informed decisions about requests for new functionality, enables more accurate and timelier estimates for work, and accelerates the design of new system functionality when projects are approved.

There are other good reasons to choose a capability-driven decomposition of the system architecture as well. Business capabilities are directly tied to business strategy. Clearly, capabilities are the source of the client's strategic differentiation and the enablers of change in the client's business. Hence, utilizing a capability-driven decomposition for the system architecture establishes a mechanism to directly link the system architecture to client business strategies. In essence, each new major capability becomes a unit of design in the system architecture.

Finally, we should note that whatever choices are made about the design of the system architecture, this design should fit in the context of existing systems in order to enhance the value of past investments. Of course, ideally, it should capture and highlight what has worked well in the past and avoid replicating what has not. Insofar as possible, it should anticipate the future, incorporating known trends and likely future scenarios. Finally, the design should also identify and exploit opportunities for reuse within the system.

Managing the System Architecture

As software systems grow in complexity, managing the system architecture becomes more demanding. Individuals who work in the architectural domain need to have gained considerable proficiency, through experience and a unique set of skills, at solving complex system-level problems. Dana Bredemeyer and Ruth Malan have observed that organizations can build competitive strength by identifying and developing the typically small group of individuals who have demonstrated through their experience and talents a particular prowess for system-level thinking about design. These individuals are typically known as architects, and their responsibility is to make architectural decisions that protect and develop the system architecture. [21]

As requirements for system development are collected and analyzed, the architects should be involved with those requirements that are deemed architecturally significant. Architecturally significant requirements are typically those that impact essential functionality of the system, have broad impact across one or more subsystems, involve significant development risks, make significant new performance demands, or have the potential to impact internal or external system communications or synchronization.

Architects also play an important role in guiding the development of the system in ways that contribute to increased efficiencies, flexibilities, or competitive advantages for the organization. For example, in reviewing multiple project requirements, the architects may observe that new features being asked for by one or more clients are similar or are likely to be of interest to other clients. Hence, a more global approach to the design of this functionality may be warranted, whereas the need for or advantage of such a global design approach would not be obvious to those working on the individual projects. On the other hand, the architects may identify conflicting requirements or requirements that are not easily accommodated by the current architecture, thus prompting a higher-level discussion about feasibility or design and implementation strategies relative to these.

Architects can also help project teams become aware of more global issues that are not an explicit part of project requirements. For example, the architects have the advantage of a higher-level view of such issues as corporate standards, IT strategic directions and initiatives, overall client business strategies and directions, and emerging new developments and trends in technology. This more global perspective allows the architects to better evaluate opportunities for innovation, overall project cost/benefits, and risks involving such issues as technological overreach and unwarranted feature explosion.

Clearly, a defining characteristic of architectural decisions is that they are made from a broad-scoped or system perspective. Any decision that can be effectively made from a more local perspective is not architectural. In other words, it is important to distinguish between detailed design and implementation decisions on the one hand, and architectural decisions on the other. Architectural decisions typically impact several different parts of the overall system, and a system-level perspective is required to take such impact into account and to analyze the various trade-offs involved.

Generally, architectural decisions concern or impact things such as system modularization, system performance and stability, global system properties, the fit of proposed changes with system design, and system conceptual integrity. While all of these are important, the issue of system conceptual integrity is often paramount. Recall that system conceptual integrity means having, or being conceived of as having, a unified overall design, form, or structure. It is a measure of the congruence of the pieces as parts of the whole. As Bredemeyer and Malan have noted, we see this concept clearly in building architecture, where architectural integrity drives structural forms such as levels, roof lines, and space layout, as well as details like the size and style of windows and other architectural trim. The goal is for the architectural decisions to result in a smoothly integrated blend of form and function, displaying balance, compatibility, and harmony among the parts, as well as an effective fit to purpose.

Given all these considerations, the organization should work out methods that optimize the architects' time. Architects are highly valuable and essential technical assets of the organization, and their expertise should be used wisely. Their attention should be focused on the truly architectural issues and decisions and not on decisions that could be made at a more detailed organizational level. This means that it is likely unrealistic for them to be expected to thoroughly review the requirements for every project the organization undertakes. Even if this were possible, it may not be desirable as this would deter the creativity, innovation, and motivation of those charged with the design and implementation of solutions at lower levels of the organization. Hence processes should be established to filter effectively what the architects are asked to review.

There is another set of decisions that the architects are also involved in. These are even higher level decisions, what can be called the *metadecision level*. These decisions set the overall architectural vision, strategy, and fundamental design principles and concepts chosen by the organization to provide a consistent approach and framework for all the organization's design activities—high-level through lower-level. These metadecisions strongly influence the integrity, design, and structure of the system, but are not in themselves decisions about the design and structure of the system. Instead, they define a framework of principles and philosophy, which in turn leads to ruling out certain design and structural choices, and guides decisions and trade-offs among others.

Such a framework makes communication about the architecture easier, because it provides a way to explain design and structure decisions. Each architectural decision made in the organization should have a well-reasoned rationale. Because architectural decisions seek to optimize system behavior and characteristics from a high-level perspective, these decisions may appear suboptimal from a more localized perspective. Providing a clear high-level rationale based on the overall architectural framework of principles and philosophy enables those with local perspective to understand these decisions better.

The architectural framework also acts as a guide to the architects as they make ongoing decisions and provides a consistent approach for these decisions. In addition, the more effectively these principles and this philosophy is communicated to developers and designers, the more they can guide design decisions at the non-architectural level as well, thus contributing to the conceptual integrity of the system at all levels. Further, such a framework provides a useful vehicle for communicating the essential nature of the architecture to non-technical audiences, such as management, marketing, and users. Finally, Joe Batman suggests that the effectiveness of such a framework is enhanced if it emphasizes a relatively small number of system principles and concepts that are focused on reducing complexity and abstracting system characteristics. This better allows designers to master these and apply them consistently to help the organization retain intellectual control of the overall system design. [22]

Chapter 6

The IT Value Challenge:
Balancing Cost and Quality

However beautiful the strategy, you should occasionally look at the results.

Winston Churchill

If an IT organization is to create a strategic advantage, it must produce results that embody value for its customers. However, among the most commonly heard complaints about IT organizations are that (1) costs are out of control, and (2) they do not deliver on their promises. The landmark Standish Group *Chaos Report*, found that only 16 percent of projects were on schedule, within budget, and delivered all the functionality promised in the project specifications.[23] Indeed, few industries have a worse record in this regard. The realities of cost and schedule overruns and undelivered functionality, or at the least strong perceptions of these *as* realities, are clear proof that IT faces a serious *value challenge.*

Of course, every successful business must address the central factors of cost, schedule, and quality (as measured by the extent to which products fulfill customer requirements) by employing effective cost measurement and control, and ensuring that the needs and demands of its customers are met in a timely manner. Simply put, any successful business must meet the challenge of delivering value to its customers. And though the precise interpretation of value is no doubt customer-specific, it always involves a mixture of the major factors of cost, schedule, and quality. Some customers are more focused on cost, others on schedule, and still others on quality, but we can be sure that all customers have specific expectations about the balance of these factors.

So it is no surprise then that this value challenge is also inherent in IT. However, it is perhaps more daunting in IT than in most other businesses. As we will see, the special nature of the value challenge in IT is driven by the unique characteristics of software, characteristics that both complicate its production and make the management of this production difficult and demanding.

Defining Quality

The *Guide to the Project Management Body of Knowledge* defines quality in terms of customer satisfaction measured against agreed-upon requirements. Quality is the degree to which a set of inherent characteristics fulfills customer requirements.[12] The International Standards Organization in its *ISO 9000 Standard* defines quality similarly as all those features of a product (or service) that are *required by the customer.* [24]

More commonly phrased definitions or descriptions of quality often focus on superiority or some measure of the grade of excellence in a product or service. However, it is important, especially in the context of delivering IT products and services, to distinguish *quality* and *grade.* Grade is a general category or rank of product or service—as in good-better-best or low-medium-high. Quality, on the other hand, should be measured by the extent to which the requirements and expectations of the customer have been satisfied. It is the customer's expressed requirements that should be used to judge the quality of a result. There is a particular danger if the customer is confused about this, because we are likely to get undesirable outcomes. Thus it is important for the customer to understand and agree to this definition of quality from the start, and setting clear acceptance criteria at the beginning of a project is a crucial step toward accomplishing this. Once we agree with our customers on what quality is and what it means on a particular project (i.e., satisfying the requirements), we must ensure that we have in place the proper production and management processes to deliver the promised quality.

Over the past fifty years, quality has come to be recognized not only as a key component of customer value but also as a major factor in enhancing productivity and thus reducing costs. As a consequence, if an organization wishes to focus on increasing productivity and reducing cost, this still requires significant attention to quality.

The Cost of Quality

The American quality pioneer Philip Crosby focused on measuring the cost of quality and introduced the phrase "quality is free" [25]. The cost of quality refers to the total cost of all efforts related to quality. This includes all work to build a product or service that conforms to the requirements, the work required to appraise the product or service for conformance to requirements, and the rework to correct any failings to meet requirements.

This description of the cost of quality includes the two broad categories of the cost: the cost of meeting the requirements, or *cost of conformance*, and the cost of not meeting requirements, or *cost of nonconformance*. The cost of conformance is the more obvious of these two categories, and for this reason it is often more closely monitored. The cost of nonconformance is at least partially hidden until the nonconformance is discovered—often late in a project or even after the product is delivered. This makes the cost of nonconformance harder to anticipate and often harder to measure accurately because it is not budgeted, but rather it is incurred to "fix" one or more problems or deficiencies. But it is nonetheless real and in many cases actually exceeds the cost of conformance on projects.

Among the costs of conformance are planning, training, process control, process validation, design validation, inspections, walkthroughs, testing, and quality audits. These represent the processes and techniques that best practice would confirm as quality success factors. Contrast these with costs of nonconformance such as rework, scrap work, complaint handling, liability judgments, product recalls, post-delivery corrective work, damaged customer relations, and in the worst case, loss of customers. Clearly these latter costs are ones that are not ordinarily built into project or organizational budgets. Because these costs are not budgeted, when they are incurred they are unexpected, and their impact on company profitability can be dramatic.

Crosby's phrase "quality is free" comes from comparing the cost of conformance to the cost of nonconformance. Examples involving serious liability issues and product recalls dramatically illustrate Crosby's basic contention. In these cases, the cost of nonconformance far outstrips the cost of building quality into the product during development. Nonconformance costs can be especially significant in software development work. Generally, in software projects, nonconformance involves considerable rework instead of actual product recalls, and rework can involve an enormous investment of effort and contribute to serious schedule delays and increased cost.

Compounding the problems with nonconformance is the fact that its associated costs can often be hard to quantify. For example, in software development projects, rework is often done by persons already on the development team and may even be mixed in with the ongoing development effort. However, even though exact costs may be difficult to assign with software, it is well documented by a number of studies that the cost to correct errors grows exponentially with the time difference between when the error is made and when it is discovered and repaired. [26] This relationship is illustrated in figure 5.1, where it is clear that the cost of rework for mistakes made in project initiation, due in large part to poor or nonexistent quality planning early on, can be devastating to a project's success.

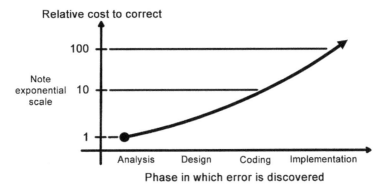

Figure 6.1: *The cost to correct errors made in analysis as a function of when they are discovered.*

For example, failure to validate a relatively simple require-ment could produce eventual costs far out of proportion to the perceived importance of the requirement to the project. A small misunderstanding that could be corrected with little effort dur-ing requirements analysis could end up involving a large redesign effort in a software module much later on in the project, costing one hundred times as much effort or more. And in extreme cases, small errors or failure to validate requirements or design details can actually render the software useless for its purpose. An infa-mous example of this occurred at NASA in 1999, when the failure to convert English measurements to metric measurements in the transfer of data between the Mars Climate Orbiter spacecraft team in Colorado and the mission navigation team in California led to software errors causing the loss of the spacecraft [27].

Issues of Ambiguity in Software

As we noted, the value challenge is perhaps more daunting in IT, especially where software development is central, than in many other businesses. Two important factors in this challenge are: a kind of *creative ambiguity* that contributes to the difficulty of measuring progress and assessing quality in the software development process, and the inevitable *communication ambiguity* that makes it all but impossible to precisely and completely specify software requirements.

Both these factors are illustrated in figure 6.2. Imagine that the speaker (i.e., the customer) is attempting to communicate in precise terms the requirements of some sort of transportation vehicle. The two listeners (i.e., solutions suppliers) are attempting to gather the speaker's "requirements" and formulate a "solution" based on these requirements. The figure could be thought of as demonstrating both types of ambiguity we just defined. First, it is possible and plausible that the two solutions providers heard very different elements of the customer's requirements. Perhaps the speaker misspoke, or perhaps the solutions providers simply misunderstood what was said—*communication ambiguity*. Second, even if they heard similar requirements, they might still have envisioned the two quite distinct solutions to the customer's problem—*creative ambiguity*.

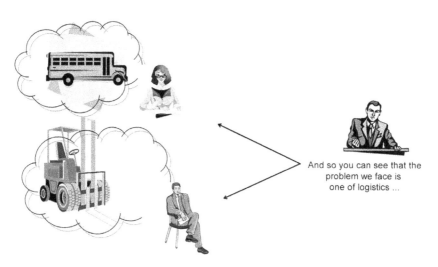

Figure 6.2: *Ambiguity in communication and visualizing "solutions."*

Of course in this particular case, it should not be that difficult to reduce the ambiguities. Because the "solution" is a tangible product, the two solutions providers could each provide the customer with a diagram, mockup, or prototype of their proposed solutions and the customer could then help resolve the ambiguities. But, as we discussed in chapter 1, software is not a tangible product. It only becomes tangible when it is executed on computer hardware, and unfortunately by that time it is difficult or impractical to refine the requirements.

Software development is a creative process and thus subject to creative ambiguity. This is reflected in the fact that software developers have many degrees of freedom in designing and implementing software that satisfies a given set of requirements. An important consequence of multiple degrees of freedom is that two developers might judge quality in the creation of a software product quite differently. Indeed, there are always many ways that creative developers can imagine to enhance or embellish a product. Requirements can be "satisfied" at various levels, and the choices involved in deciding what level to implement are subtle and subject to interpretation and disagreement among those responsible for the implementation.

Communication ambiguities also contribute to the value challenge for an IT business. The fact is that customers are most often unable to articulate precisely the requirements for a software project. This happens because of a natural and unavoidable communication gap between customers and those who implement IT solutions to customer problems and needs. This gap arises partly because customers and developers speak different "languages." The customer describes needs or problems in the language of the relevant business environment. The developer must then translate these articulated needs into the language of a technical system that can realize the solution of the stated problems. Not unexpectedly, this translation is often flawed. We shouldn't rush to place the blame on either party. Communication involves both the transmitting and the receiving of information. Care must be exercised in *both* directions for good communications.

Further, in software development, communication ambiguity and creative ambiguity are often intertwined. There is no unique technical solution to the customer's problems—even if they are perfectly understood. Moving from a problem to a solution involves not only a translation into a different kind of language but also envisioning and choosing a potential solution approach from the many that are possible.

But there is an even more fundamental issue at the heart of the matter, and that is the inherent ambiguity and lack of precision in all human communication about abstract concepts. In Michael Frayn's play *Copenhagen*, the two physicists Werner Heisenberg and Niels Bohr find it impossible (even in the afterlife) to agree on what was said at a meeting the two had in Copenhagen in 1941. The play is based on an actual meeting that did take place in Copenhagen, and the real Bohr and Heisenberg did disagree greatly afterward about what was said during the meeting (except to agree that the meeting was about nuclear fission).

Quantum physics is the theoretical basis of modern physics that explains the nature and behavior of matter and energy on the atomic and subatomic level. Heisenberg articulated the famous uncertainty principle in quantum physics, which states that locating a particle in a small region of space makes the momentum of the particle uncertain; and conversely, that measuring the momentum of a particle precisely makes the position uncertain. In other words, the simultaneous position and momentum that define a particle in classical physics are *inherently and irresolvably ambiguous.* The play dramatizes the analogy between Heisenberg's uncertainty principle and the inability to derive the precise meaning of any human communication.

The Peculiar Nature of Software

We can draw other parallels between quantum physics and software development. The parallels are rooted in the shared creative processes between physics and software development, not unlike the shared creative processes between art and software development. However, there is a primary difference between the creativity applied to physics and that applied to art. Creativity in physics is bound by the realities of nature. In contrast, creativity in art is bound only by the human imagination. As we see in this section, creativity in software is akin to creativity in physics in that it is bound by important underlying realities.

Why are the concepts of quantum physics so hard for most of us to grasp? The primary reason is that the vast majority of our direct experiences and observations about the world are at the macroscopic level, where the world appears to abide by the laws of classical physics. In other words, our intuition is derived from and based almost exclusively on classical physics or *intuitive realities*. However, that intuition misleads us at almost every turn in the quantum world, and thus we must approach quantum physics by recognizing the existence of *nonintuitive realities* that determine the quantum world's behavior. As we will see, just as quantum physics explores the peculiar world of atomic and subatomic phenomena, software exhibits its own peculiar nature.

A similar *clash between intuition and reality* occurs in software development. Some of the realities of nature are easily observed, but subatomic quantum phenomena can only be deduced by creative analysis of indirect measurements. The underlying realities of software development must be similarly deduced from our creative analysis of indirect observations of the abstraction of software through its tangible behavior on computer hardware.

One of the most frequent clashes between intuition and reality in software development is in customer expectations of the software process and its results. In today's typical business environment, we have computers on every desk. These computers have capabilities that were unimaginable twenty years ago. Furthermore, they are connected to a network of computers that are capable of almost instant access to an amazing range of information. So the expectations of customers concerning their computing power and convenience—based legitimately enough on their own experiences—are high. Customers are apt to have little patience with the harsh realities of software development—a process with which few have any experience.

For example, in the customer view, software projects take far longer than they should because customers have come to believe that creativity should occur at warp speed. If a project falls behind schedule, customers see a simple solution in adding more people to the project to get it back on schedule. Customers also expect developers to design and build systems that are fully featured and complex, and satisfy all requirements both stated and implied. In addition, they expect these systems to take full advantage of changes in technology to be technically current. Unfortunately, none of these expectations match the reality of software development.

Hardware productivity improvement occurs at an exponential pace. Moore's Law, which states that hardware speed and capacity double roughly every eighteen to twenty-four months, has proven true over the past few decades. [28] We have seen the number of transistors and resistors on a chip double at essentially this rate. In 1965 a typical chip contained the equivalent of sixty such devices; by 2005 this number was almost two billion devices per chip! It is natural and intuitive that people would assume similar rates of improvement in software development. But the reality is that human conceptual capacity, on which software development depends, improves linearly (if at all), not exponentially.

Further, it may seem intuitive that adding people to a project would decrease its development time, but this is not the case. Putting more people on a project requires assimilation, training, management, and communication that often overshadows potential improvement in productivity. Even when these factors can be successfully managed, ten people often cannot resolve and implement logical complexity that much faster than one or two people. Human conceptual understanding is the limiting factor, not manpower [1].

Designing and delivering fully featured, complex systems that satisfy all requirements "out of the box" is a seductive goal, but it is not one that matches software development reality. A system in its initial development rarely lives up to the ideals of perfection and completion. The difficulties in this issue are often compounded by the software developers themselves, who by the demanding nature of their craft tend to be perfectionists. As we noted earlier, a 99.99

percent correctness standard works well in many industries but can be disastrous in software development. Software developers know this and develop a perfectionist approach to their work. This can lead to developers trying to create software that satisfies all imaginable requirements. In reality, this matters far less than customers may think. Rather, to be successful, the systems need only deliver the specified business requirements at implementation. Nonetheless, customers do not often understand this and hence their expectations are often unsatisfied.

In a similar way, designing systems that take full advantage of changes in technology, so that the delivered systems are always technically current, is not a realistic goal. Software project requirements are written for target technology platforms. Many software projects take months or even years to develop and deploy. During this time, Moore's Law is at work in the hardware realm; thus even if the target technology platform was current when the development project started, it is dated when the product is delivered. This is unavoidable if the project is to be delivered on schedule. Software projects that frequently change technological direction *almost never get delivered.*

Following our analogy, we could say that customers live in a "classical physics" world while software is developed in a "quantum physics" world. In other words, the experience and intuition on which customers base their expectations simply do not match the underlying realities of the software development world. This *understanding gap* is the cause of much angst in the software development industry, as software developers (being perfectionists) try to "fix" the expectation gap that this creates by themselves, ignoring the realities that they know apply to software projects. A better approach, although not an easy one, is to educate customers to a higher level of understanding of software development realities. This should be the task of software development managers, customer relationship professionals, and industry leaders.

Returning to our analogy, one of the most fundamental and non-intuitive aspects of quantum physics is that light behaves like both a particle and a wave. This apparent paradox defies and frustrates ordinary intuition, which is based on our experiences with the macro-world. There is a kind of parallel to this duality in software development. As we noted earlier, software is a product of the human imagination, or in Brooks' term, pure *thought-stuff*— an abstraction. But software is also identified with the behavior of the computer hardware on which it is implemented. Software may well be the only pure thought-stuff that has a tangible duality, namely the practical and predictable results it produces when run. Hence, people are misled about software's true complex nature; they think of it as a tangible, not abstract, creation.

Another defining feature of large software products is that they are "systems" created incrementally over time. These systems become increasingly complex during this incremental process. To be successful, the architecture of software systems must remain coherent to a single mind, even though they are designed, built, and maintained by many minds. It is important to remember that such systems are entirely a construct of the human mind—abstractions built on other abstractions. Yet, most products we deal with are not abstractions. Indeed, as we just noted, even our experience with software is through its concrete instantiation as hardware behavior. People who do not work in software development have little intuition, experience, or knowledge about the process of producing working abstractions; their understanding about the abstraction that is software is inherently flawed.

Consider, for example, a concrete object like a bridge or building. Each has a natural sequence of dependencies of construction in the physical world that a person can observe and model relatively easily. People have a natural and intuitive understanding of the basic construction process as well as the final form and function of the product. It is natural for people to use their experience with the building of tangible products to create their expectations of the development of abstract software systems in a way similar to how people apply classical physics intuition to try to understand the quantum world—with the same predictable, unavoidable disconnect.

The abstract nature of software makes it difficult for customers to fully understand its inherent difficulty. It is quite natural for them to question its high costs, why it takes so long, and why it doesn't offer all possible functionalities. There is nothing tangible for them to "see" to give them an appreciation of what was involved in its construction. Indeed, any two programs "look alike" when they are instantiated on the hardware duality. The differences in the complexity of the two programs are not at all apparent. As a contrast, recall our doghouse-skyscraper analogy from chapter 4, where the differences in the products and the complexity, effort, and challenges that went into their construction are obvious to all.

Another non-intuitive aspect of quantum physics is the uncertainty principle we mentioned earlier in our discussion. This principle captures an inescapable underlying reality of the quantum-scale world, namely that the act of observing a quantum particle changes it. In other words, we can't "determine" everything about the particle in its quantum state. To do so requires that we observe it—and the observation changes it. Once again, there is an analogy in the software development world. We write requirements for software, which is pure *thought-stuff*—an abstraction. We validate these requirements by observation of the concrete instantiation of the software on computer hardware, and this observation often "changes" the requirements. In other words, there is an uncertainty principle of sorts at work that says the true nature of the requirements will not be known until the abstraction is instantiated (observed) on hardware.

The outcome of this uncertainty is that writing complete, correct requirements for a pure abstraction is difficult, if not impossible. Note that this goes beyond the communication problems associated with requirements gathering that we discussed earlier. Those are still present as well, making it difficult to "observe" the requirements in the first place; but once we have done this, there is the additional uncertainty that can only be resolved when the software becomes concrete on hardware. Prototyping can help us with this dilemma, but of course it applies to only a limited number of types of applications and features.

One way to gain some insight into the uncertainty principle in quantum physics is the association of a probability density function with a particle. According to this interpretation, a particle may be in many different states "at the same time," the likelihood of particular states being governed by the particle's probability density function. The particle is then "assigned to a particular state" when it is observed. Hence an apparently simple entity (the location of a particle at a given time) is vastly more complex than it appears. Again, the ability to be potentially in many states at once defies ordinary intuition. We can draw an analogy to this in the software world in the area of testing.

At any given point in a program's code, the program has many different possible *logical states* depending on the particular logical path chosen through the program to get to that point. In other words, just knowing what line of code on which we are focused is not sufficient to know the state of the program at that point. As a consequence, to completely test the specific piece of code, we must test all possible logical states for a program. This is a practical impossibility because the combinatorial explosion of the number of possible states for even a moderately complex program is *unimaginably large.* To give a simple example, a program with a total of thirty simple *if...then* constructs has 2^{30} or over one billion possible logical states. If we double the number of *if...then* constructs to sixty, the program has 2^{60} possible logical states. This exponential growth rate produces astonishing results. The rather benign looking number 2^{60}—measuring states for a relatively simple program—is larger than the estimated number of grains of sand on all the beaches in the world! [30]

The consequence of this is that *all but the simplest* programs must remain incompletely tested. Instead, we rely on choosing a good sampling of test cases. Well-chosen, this sampling covers most of the important cases that we might expect to come up in practice. But no moderately large program can be tested to guarantee it against logical error, and in fact the vast majority of programs—even well-tested ones—have residual errors. This goes against ordinary intuition, which would dictate that all possible cases should be tested and that completely error-free programs should be delivered.

Our final quantum physics analogy involves the concept of *entanglement.* Entanglement in quantum physics describes a situation in which the states of two particles are inherently linked.

For entangled particles, if one's state is altered, the other's state is altered instantaneously, and this occurs even if the particles are separated by an arbitrary distance! This "action at a distance" defies ordinary intuition and was an aspect of quantum physics that even Einstein had great difficulty accepting. The related property of software is logical coupling. Logical coupling between program segments and components can be unpredictable, and it is not uncommon for a change in one part of a system to cause unintended side effects in a different part of the system—*action at a distance*! This happens when two program components are inadvertently logically coupled in some way (often through data). Although we attempt to avoid logical coupling, it is difficult, if not impossible, to ensure that it never happens.

Logical coupling has significant consequences. Customers have little understanding of the concept of logical coupling, and this causes them to fail to understand how a "minor" change can result in drastic impacts in other parts of a large system. On a practical level, they do not appreciate the need for, or the difficulty and effort involved in, effective regression testing to make sure that logical coupling does not produce such impacts. Hence they have no understanding of the true cost of "small" changes to software. This leads them to believe that software developers are being unreasonable in their estimates of the time and cost required to implement such changes, which to them seem minor or even trivial.

Much has been written over the past several decades about the so-called *software crisis*. The documented fact that software projects have proved difficult has been viewed and advertised as a *crisis* in our software development methodologies and techniques. To some extent, both the customer community and the developer community have bought into this conclusion. However, an alternate interpretation is that there is no crisis of methodologies and techniques but rather a serious understanding gap about the true realities and difficulties inherent in software development. In this interpretation, the primary reason for the observed software development difficulties is that software development is, quite frankly, *hard*. Its difficulty stems not from deficient methodologies and development tools, but from the underlying and inescapable peculiar realities of software described here.

Finally, these are not primarily philosophical issues; they have important practical impacts. The IT industry has been viewed negatively because of its track record in producing the value that customers expect. Our conclusion is that improving this record may depend at least as much on resolving the disconnect between IT customers' intuition-based perceptions and the underlying realities of software development, as it does on improved methodologies and development techniques.

Software development is plagued by unrealistic expectations because the intuition of the customer is very often at odds with the underlying realities. As we have demonstrated, this disconnect leads to unrealistic expectations about the speed of software development, the cost of software development, the degree of perfection possible in software products, the possible use of the absolute latest technology in software, the completeness and corrections of software requirements, the effectiveness of testing in producing error-free software, and the magnitude of the impact of "small" changes to software.

This understanding gap is hard to close because to do so involves educating the customer about the non-intuitive underlying realities of software, and this requires considerable effort and commitment. To make progress, we should switch the focus from trying to "solve an implementation crisis" to the challenge of better educating, over time, our customers and users about the underlying realities of software. A related challenge is to make sure the developers clearly understand the relevant business environment. (We discuss this in chapter 7.)

These considerations have important implications for those who manage software development. Understanding the peculiar nature of software enables IT managers to better focus their continuous improvement efforts on areas where those efforts can produce appropriate return on investment. At the same time, this understanding can help these managers avoid frustration in applying resources in attempts to modify the underlying, and immutable, realities of the software development process.

Managing the Balance for Value

Although developing software is certainly not quantum physics, there are some lessons to be learned from this analogy. As we have seen, a completely unambiguous precise software requirement is unattainable, thus the communication gap we have described is unavoidable. As a consequence of this gap, there are often additional requirements, or at least significantly changing requirements, that emerge during a software development project.

When these changes are discovered, the technical team implementing the project wants to satisfy all these additional requirements—and maybe add a few more enhancements that come up in the design process. Software developers, who are trained to create effective solutions and who find great satisfaction in doing just that, naturally focus on the ultimate effectiveness of the solutions they are creating.

Because software developers are focused on creating the most effective product for the customer, it is not uncommon to run over schedule and over budget. This would be predictable in almost any creative process if the creative forces were not constrained and managed well. Successful software development must put in place checks and balances that adequately control expenditures of money and time. Software developers are typically not the best judges of either of these during a project because they are more likely to focus on creating and delivering an effective solution.

The metaphor in figure 6.3 illustrates this tension. The value sought in this case is as swift a trip downstream as possible. If the crew is to achieve its goal, rowing must be balanced. If too much effort is placed on either side of the boat, it veers off its optimal path, requiring adjustments to put it back on track. In a worse case, the boat may veer onto rocks or into the riverbank, preventing the boat from completing the journey at all. Note that the crew is facing in the opposite direction of the boat's motion and totally immersed in the job at hand. The person sitting in front of the crew and facing toward the motion of the boat is called the coxswain. It is the coxswain's responsibility to monitor the boat's direction and make adjustments before such drastic outcomes occur. In other words, a well-defined process is in place to ensure the balance necessary for a successful outcome.

Figure 6.3: *Achieving success requires a well-defined process for maintaining balance of effort.*

So it is with software development. Those charged with the efficiency and effectiveness of the effort are focused on their aspect of the task at hand. Indeed, managing cost and schedule in software development requires a sharp focus on efficiency, and creating quality requires a sharp focus on effectiveness. The tension between these two is inevitable, but achieving a proper balance between them is what delivers the desired value to the customer. Achieving this balance requires well-defined, repeatable management processes for imposing the necessary constraints on the software development processes. These management processes should also include the capabilities necessary to set and adjust priorities—both among projects and within the work on individual projects—as well as the framework for orderly escalation of issues to guarantee the requisite product and process quality.

Part III
Creating Client Value

Chapter 7

Meeting the Value Challenge:
Focusing on IT as a Business

Don't dissipate your powers; strive to concentrate them. Genius thinks it can do whatever it sees others doing, but it will surely repent of every ill-judged outlay.

Goethe

In chapter 6, we discussed the need to balance cost (efficiency) and quality (effectiveness) to produce value for customers, and we saw how the nature of software development makes this especially difficult for an IT company. Indeed, the peculiar nature of software combined with the difficulty of managing a highly creative workforce forms the essence of the management challenge confronting all IT companies. Both factors—the difficult nature of software and the creativity of the workforce—produce forces that dissipate energy and resources. Dissipation clearly works against containing costs, but it can result in diluted quality as well. So a central theme in delivering value to customers is to achieve and maintain a sharp focus against the natural tendencies toward resource dissipation present in an IT environment.

Maintaining such a focus is the central step toward *running IT as a business.* To run IT as a business, managers must be exposed to and institutionalize the common business practices and governance under which non-IT business functions operate, in order to accurately measure and communicate costs, which are critical steps in achieving IT efficiency. However, managers are also responsible for making IT effective, which is achieved through a continued focus on their technical competence that allows them to successfully manage technical operations and provide information for capacity planning and resource allocation. The need for this focus is just as critical in IT organizations that are housed within larger organizations as it is in stand-alone IT companies. Organizations within a larger business should no longer be viewed as a cost center within the larger business but must operate as a business within that business. In effect, IT must be managed as a profitable business—or at the least as a zero-cost business—within a business.

In this context, IT managers find themselves with no shortage of major and conflicting challenges. For example, the expanding complexity of rapidly evolving technologies can work against the need to increase productivity and contain costs. Increasing demands are emerging for 24-7, high-performance application services to support customers' global business initiatives. Customer satisfaction must be protected and enhanced through superior user experiences and effective service level agreements in the face of changing business requirements, stiff competition, and the emergence of trends like utility computing. And cost effectiveness must be achieved and maintained through accurate chargeback accounting that enables better control of budgets and schedules.

At a higher organizational level, strategies must be carefully crafted in the face of a multitude of perceived opportunities and possibilities. The IT landscape changes rapidly, and one of the challenges of running IT as a business is to balance change and continuity. As we noted earlier, Drucker maintains that the successful companies of the future will be change leaders, but at the same time he emphasizes that becoming a change leader is best accomplished by an evolutionary approach. So overall focus must be carefully balanced to ensure the energy and resources to pursue of the right kind of change, while providing the necessary restraint in the face of opportunities that almost always exceed organizational resources.

Establishing and Maintaining Strategic Focus

Meeting the kinds of challenges just described requires a plethora of decisions, and some of these decisions could easily be at odds with one another. To avoid this happening, these challenges need to be addressed in a continuous systemic manner, rather than as individual problem-solving episodes. The organization must approach decision making within a clearly defined framework to consistently hit value targets. As we discussed earlier, one way to establish such a decision-making framework is to adopt a model-based approach to managing the organization.

The IT-OSD model we described provides one such example, in which strategies are driven by a clear understanding of the organization's mission and its guiding principles. But even within such a model, the IT organization must still act wisely in establishing and maintaining its strategic focus. The *hedgehog concept* introduced by Jim Collins in his book *Good to Great* provides a vehicle for accomplishing that.

In his study of companies that made the transition from good to great, Collins found characteristics that these companies seemed to have in common. One of the most important was the ability to focus on the things that supported their success, while at the same time eliminating or avoiding those things that had the potential to dissipate resources and that were unlikely to make major contributions to the company's success.

Collins articulated these ideas using philosopher Isaiah Berlin's famous metaphor of the hedgehog and the fox. While Berlin used the metaphor in an attempt to classify thinkers and writers, Collins has adapted it to organizations. A fox appears to be a sly, clever, and curious animal that explores and pursues many ideas. On the other hand, a hedgehog seems to simplify complex issues into a single organizing principle that unifies everything else and provides guidance at all times. Everything that does not relate directly to this organizing principle is considered irrelevant. The hedgehog exhibits this behavior when it curls into a tight ball in the presence of danger.

Foxes seem to appreciate the complexity of the world and attempt to incorporate it into their decision making. While admirable to a point, this approach has the danger of leading to a lack of focus and the absence of a unifying vision. On the other hand, hedgehogs adopt a different approach, evaluating options within a simpler and more structured framework, separating those factors relevant for the pursuit at hand from those that, while interesting, bear no direct relevance to this pursuit.

The hedgehog's simplicity of framework can help organizations better understand which outcomes they should pursue and how to organize their limited resources within this pursuit. Indeed, in his research, Collins discovered that the good-to-great companies behaved much more like hedgehogs than foxes. These companies built their vision and developed their strategies around a simple and focused business model encapsulated in the organization's *hedgehog concept.*

An organization's hedgehog concept can be identified by answering the following three questions.

1. What can the organization be best in the world at (and as a corollary, what can it *not* be best at)?

2. What is the organization deeply passionate about?

3. What drives the organization's economic engine?

A company's hedgehog concept is found where the answers to these three questions intersect. The diagram in figure 7.1 illustrates this idea. The diagram can help an organization make fundamental choices that create and maintain focus. For example, deciding which customers to pursue and which needs of these customers the organization possesses the particular and differentiating expertise, capability, and passion to satisfy is a critical evaluation for any organization. The organization's hedgehog concept can help make this evaluation more realistically in terms of the organization's expertise, passion, and economic engine.

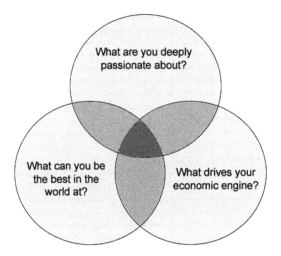

Figure 7.1: *The three circles of the Hedgehog Concept.*

Of the three dimensions involved in the hedgehog concept, the one that is perhaps least under the organization's control is the economic engine. The economic engine must be measured by metrics created outside the organization, and these metrics should translate into the things valued by the broader economic environment in which the organization operates. The economic engine provides the adjustment to an organization's focus to ensure economic success.

As figure 7.2 illustrates, the intersection of the circles representing an organization's passion and its best-in-world expertise provides an *excellence zone* inside which the organization should be able to perform at a high level—doing what it is best at and doing it with passion! But performing excellently in a region of the excellence zone that does not deliver economic benefits is not a desired goal for a business organization. Hence the organization will want to find, and focus its activities in, a smaller area within the excellence zone that does produce economic benefit. The third circle, which reflects the identification of an appropriate economic engine, provides the organization the ability to identify this optimal area of focus—the intersection of *three* circles, which is the organization's *economic success zone*. The economic engine, therefore, enables the organization to identify how it can best use its expertise and its passion to achieve and sustain economic success.

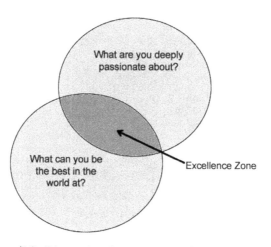

Figure 7.2: *Discovering the organization's Excellence Zone.*

It is important to emphasize that the hedgehog concept represents an *understanding* of what an organization can be best at and what it has great passion for. It is not a goal to be the best, not a strategy to be the best, not a plan to be the best, nor is it a decision about where the organization's passion will lie. It is deeper than that. The organization's fundamental expertise, talent, and passion are characteristics that *already exist.* Hence, the hedgehog concept is not something that is typically determined in a short period of time. It is not even something that an organization can define at a moment in time, but it is rather something intrinsic that must be discovered over time. Once discovered, it can be a powerful insight to guide the development of strategies and the commitment of resources. This is not to say that elements of the hedgehog can't change over time. But given the importance of the hedgehog as an overriding organizing principle, the wise organization approaches such change cautiously and with deep analysis.

Often beyond the organization's control, economic engines *can* shift over time and new economic engines with their associated opportunities appear. The shifting of economic engines or the appearance of potential new economic engines can occur for any number of reasons, including changing customer demand, new government regulations, the emergence of a strong competitor with a new business model, demographic factors, new approaches to outsourcing, and so forth. If a company understands its hedgehog concept, it is better positioned to evaluate its possible courses of action in both these major circumstances—the shifting of an existing economic engine and the appearance of a potential new economic engine.

In either of these situations, four different cases might apply relative to a company's hedgehog concept as illustrated in figure 7.3. In case (a), the new or shifted economic engine is outside the company's area of expertise and its passion. Clearly in this case, any pursuit of the related opportunities based on this economic engine would be highly unlikely to result in success. To be successful, the company would have to change both its expertise and its passion. Changing either of these would be daunting by itself, but changing both would be all but impossible. In case (b), there is an overlap of the new economic engine and the company's passion but not with its expertise. So while the related opportunities may appear attractive, the capability to pursue them successfully is lacking.

In case (c), there is an overlap of the new economic engine and the company's expertise but not with its passion. It may seem reasonable for the company to pursue the related opportunities, but if the company clearly understands its passion and realizes that the opportunities presented are outside that passion, it may be wise to reconsider. Although some short-term success might be achieved in this case, unless the needed passion can be generated, long-term success is questionable at best. In the final case shown in (d), the new opportunities lie within the intersection of the company's expertise and passion—what we called its excellence zone. Clearly this situation presents a good chance for success.

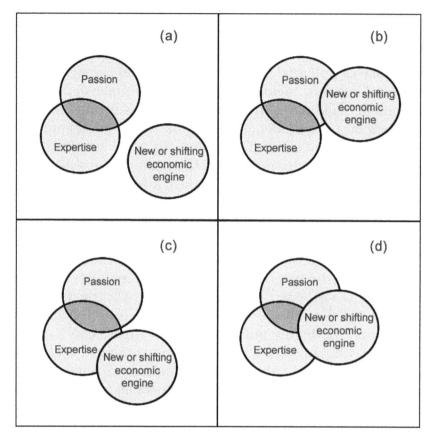

Figure 7.3: *Analyzing shifting or new economic engines.*

A major factor in (d) is whether the economic engine being considered is actually a new one or a shifted version of the company's existing economic engine. If it is a shifted version of the current economic engine, then the company would almost surely try to make the adjustments within its excellence zone to maintain its existing success. The organization's hedgehog provides a crucial framework within which to craft these adjustments. On the other hand, if the economic engine is actually a new one, then any decisions would need to take into account available resources and potential impact on the company's current successes. If the company is in a strong financial position, it may have the resources to pursue the new opportunities while continuing its current business full speed. And if analysis shows that a failure to pursue the new opportunities could have a negative impact on the company's current successes, moving to pursue these opportunities takes on more urgency.

It is beyond our scope to pursue all the nuances of a decision in any of these situations, but suffice it to say that an understanding of its hedgehog concept would prove invaluable to the company in these considerations. In cases (a)–(c), this understanding could prevent the company from making a serious error in pursuing opportunities that are not a match for its expertise or passion. In case (d), this understanding can guide the company's considerations in ways that could be the difference between its continuing success and its failure.

An example illustrates this last point. In his book *The Innovator's Dilemma,* Clayton Christensen introduced the concept of *disruptive technologies.* Disruptive technologies are emerging technologies that can appeal to or even create new markets. Such technologies are often characterized by inferior performance and low cost, at least in their early stages. These two characteristics make these technologies unattractive to successful companies who are more focused on the *sustaining technologies* that can be employed to improve their products or services to better meet their existing customers' needs. Another way to phrase this would be to say that disruptive technologies do not fit into a successful company's current economic engine model. [29]

However, such technologies might indeed present a potential new economic engine for a company. Of course, there may be—in fact typically will be—many new technologies that should be analyzed in this context. Only a few, if any, of these emerging technologies prove to have significant impact on a successful company, and there are surely never enough resources to explore them all seriously enough to discover definitively which ones these might be. On the other hand, ignoring them all can prove fatal, as Christensen's study demonstrated conclusively. So, how can the organization make wise choices about technologies to explore? A good understanding of the organization's excellence zone is a good first step in this direction.

If the potential emerging economic engine does not intersect the organization's excellence zone, it is likely that any resources spent exploring it will be wasted. But if there is an intersection with the organization's excellence zone, the exploration may be worth it because the organization has both the expertise and the potential passion to pursue opportunities successfully. Of course, the development of the emerging economic engine requires a strong market for the related product or services. But in the case this does occur, the organization's explorations may well position it to take a leadership position in that market.

In his study, Christensen cited the collapse of the mini-computer companies—Digital Equipment Company (DEC), Wang, Honeywell, and others—in the late 1980s and early 1990s. The primary driver of this collapse proved to be the unexpected and rapid emergence of the personal computer and its development into a viable business computing option. It is interesting to conjecture about what might have happened if DEC (or any of the other mini-computer companies) had taken an earlier interest in the personal computer and created its own capacity in advance of the exploding personal computer market. DEC surely had the expertise in place to become a world leader in personal computer manufacturing. One would also assume that the passion for doing so was either in place or could likely have been developed. In other words, the emerging economic engine of the personal computer market would have likely intersected DEC's excellence zone. Perhaps, if DEC's managers had been more sensitive to the organization's hedgehog, they might have pursued the related opportunities and the course of the company's history could have been different.

Establishing and Maintaining Tactical Focus

The ideas we have discussed thus far can help an IT organization establish, evaluate, and maintain its overall focus. The hedgehog concept can help establish which products and services are compatible with its excellence zone. In essence, it helps determine the kind of work to be pursued and discourages the organization from dissipating resources on work outside its excellence zone that will likely prove unsuccessful in the long term. However, to run IT as a business requires that this focus permeate the entire organization.

In an IT organization, the majority of the workforce is engaged in projects and smaller levels-of-effort that articulate, design, and build IT products and services. Earlier we mentioned the Standish Group's landmark *1994 CHAOS Report*. The *CHAOS Report* was based on a survey of 360 IT executives who reported on over 8,000 IT projects. The executives were asked to evaluate how the various projects they were reporting on measured up relative to budget, schedule, and functionality provided to the customer. The results were both surprising and discouraging. The Standish researchers identified three types of projects:

- *Successful projects.* The project was completed on time and on budget, with essentially all features and functions as initially specified.

- *Challenged projects.* The project was completed and operational, but with one or more of the following characteristics: over-budget, over-schedule, delivered fewer features and functions than originally specified.

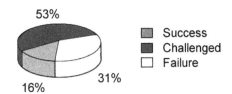

Figure 7.4: *IT project success rates from the CHAOS Report.*

- *Failed projects.* The project was canceled at some point during its development.

The percentages of projects in these three categories are shown in figure 7.4. Subsequent studies confirm the general conclusions of the original *CHAOS Report.* There was much room for improvement in success rates for IT projects. Indeed, to run IT as a successful business demands considerable improvement.

Project Focus

The Standish Group asked the executives to list the most important success factors for projects in their experience. They cited the following four leading factors (with the percentage of executives listing these) in the 1994 study:

1. User involvement (16%)

2. Executive management support (14%)

3. Clear requirements (13%)

4. Proper planning (10%)

Achieving these success factors requires a sharp focus within the project itself—especially early on in the project. All are issues of good project management.

The IT industry has been late to embrace the importance of the discipline of project management. This is especially the case in software development, where those performing the technical work of analysis and design often manage the project too. However, over the past decade or so, there has been an increasing awareness in the industry of both the importance of the project management discipline and the different responsibilities involved in managing the project and the work to create the product.

The Project Management Institute, the world's largest professional organization devoted to the discipline, defines project management as "the application of knowledge, skills, tools, and techniques to project activities to meet project requirements." Although this definition is quite succinct, it captures the most important features of the discipline of project management.

Right up front, the definition establishes the discipline as an applied discipline—"the application of." The discipline is multifaceted and involves "knowledge, skills, tools, and techniques." In particular, it has both a conceptual and an applied nature, and its practice requires a wide spectrum or range of skills. The discipline's skills are applied to "activities" within the project. Projects require work or activities and project management involves the application of knowledge and skills to these activities. And finally the activities are sharply focused on meeting project requirements.

Most projects focus on producing a product (including services)—sometimes new, sometimes modified from an existing product. Most every product is produced by an associated development process that typically follows a life cycle and a related methodology. It is then important within this context to distinguish between the project management and product development processes. The two types of work, while related, operate at different organizational levels.

For example, if we assume that the product to be produced is a software product, the overall development process is usually referred to as the software development life cycle. Within this life cycle, there are environment-specific processes and work-product deliverables that are referred to as a methodology. Methodologies are often modeled after industry best practices, with tailoring for a specific company environment.

Project management is intended to complement, reinforce, and facilitate the methodology and software development life cycle—but not to interfere with, hamper, or replace these in any way. Facilitating and enabling tasks are the main focus of project management. Project management ensures that the product development processes function efficiently and effectively. In the successful software development environment, the project management and software development processes integrate smoothly and seamlessly. Project management is a set of *umbrella processes* that overlay the software development life cycle and methodology, as figure 7.5 illustrates.

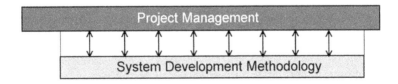

Figure 7.5: *The relationship between Project Management and System Development.*

The aim of project management is to maintain the project's focus relative to its schedule, its budget, and its objectives—sometimes referred to as the triple constraints of project management. While the hedgehog concept ensures that the organization is doing the correct projects relative to the organization's business goals, project management ensures that those projects are managed well for the realization of those business goals.

Requirements Focus

As the Standish *CHAOS Report* demonstrates, perhaps IT project management's greatest challenge is to ensure that project requirements reflect the project's true objectives and that they are articulated at a level of detail and completeness that allows developers to deliver the required products and services. The following example illustrates this dramatically.

In 2004, the FBI's planned automated case management system was abandoned after $170 million had been spent on its development! One of the authors of the U.S. General Accounting Office report on the failed project summarized its difficulties:

> It was a classic case of not getting the requirements sufficiently defined in terms of completeness and correctness from the beginning. And so it required *a continuous redefinition of requirements that had a cascading effect on what had already been designed and produced* (emphasis added).

This cascading effect was largely due to rework. In software development, rework is especially expensive because software is typically a highly integrated and logically interconnected entity. As we saw in the last chapter, the cost to correct errors grows exponentially as a function of the time between discovery and correction. Even small changes in the requirements can cause a great deal of rework when discovered late in the process.

Why is meeting this challenge so difficult, and how can organizations improve their chances of meeting it? We earlier identified the peculiar nature of software and part of this peculiarity has to do with the difficulty of articulating project requirements. These underlying difficulties are real and won't disappear no matter what we do. However, on a practical level, we can identify some fundamental principles of requirements that have direct impact on resources in any IT organization.

Seven Principles of Requirements Management

No matter how well the IT organization understands and communicates its overall focus, if those implementing the organization's strategies do not understand and apply the principles of requirements, resources are dissipated and the battle for balance between cost and quality can be lost on the front lines. The following seven important principles can help an organization maintain the proper focus on requirements management.

Principle #1: Bad Requirements Lead to Unsuccessful Projects

Requirements drive all other aspects of a project. If the requirements are incorrect or incomplete, no matter how perfect the design and implementation, the results do not meet customer expectations. When this happens, resources are wasted, and, worse yet, customer relationships are been damaged with possible serious consequences.

Successful projects are realized only when the customer's needs and expectations are met. However, the actual project work is directed by the project requirements. Thus for success, the customer's needs and expectations must be accurately reflected in the requirements. In other words, great projects result from good implementation and execution based on great requirements. The flip side of this is that bad requirements lead to unsuccessful projects—no matter how flawless the work in the rest of the project.

When a project has bad requirements, even if the correct requirements are eventually discovered, the cost and time required to implement them may be so excessive that the customer is not satisfied. Meeting the customer's needs and expectations for system functionality may not guarantee a successful project when project costs and delivery times are far over estimates. Major drivers of customer expectations are the cost and time estimates made at the beginning of the project. The effects of missing or misunderstood requirements always produces projects over-budget and over-schedule, and so even if the deficiencies in the requirements are discovered and repaired, the projects may be deemed unsuccessful.

Principle #2: Requirements Must Be Discovered, Not Just Gathered

Customers do not think of everything they need to tell the requirements analysts, nor are they able to communicate them easily. Customers may not even have a good understanding of the problem they are seeking to solve. Those involved in requirements articulation should view themselves as consultants and problem solvers whose job is to help the customer to discover the true problem and articulate a good solution.

What the customer often has analyzed are a set of symptoms that have expressed themselves, and it is the requirements analyst's job to dig deeper and get to the root problem. At the beginning of analysis, the problem is only partly formed—even though the customer may think it is well-defined.

Once the true problem has been identified, understood, and framed correctly, it must be articulated precisely to ensure that the customer shares this understanding. Once the problem is agreed on, the requirements analysts must work diligently to capture requirements that ensure a solution acceptable to the customer.

The fundamental task is to move from the problem to a set of system requirements to solve the problem. This involves a process of discovery and is almost never a matter of simply gathering the requirements. Together with the customer, the requirements analyst must probe and analyze to define the unspoken or poorly articulated requirements with which most projects begin.

Principle #3: Requirements Discovery Is a Process, Not an Event

Requirements discovery is an iterative process. Requirements must be articulated and validated with the customer, and then the whole process must be repeated. Taking things at face value after one customer meeting or communication is a sure way to produce incorrect and incomplete requirements and may even lead to an attempt to solve the wrong problem completely.

Because requirements must be discovered and not simply gathered, it is important to realize that discovery is a process and not an event. It involves trial and error. The requirements analyst must ask probing questions, formulate requirements statements on the basis of the answers, and then validate these requirements statements with the customer and users.

This process is usually more effective if it is done over some reasonable period of time. Requirements analysts need time to study information they have collected in order to formulate and articulate requirements. Customers and users must have time in turn to think through the proposed requirements and make certain that they capture the appropriate and correct needs and expectations of the various stakeholders.

Human communication is an error-prone and difficult process on all levels. These difficulties are even more pronounced when the subject matter is itself complex—as is the case for most IT projects. An iterative approach usually has the best chance of success, despite the pressure of time that is often present in such projects. The extra time needed for the iterative approach can be time well spent when you consider the cost curve we studied earlier.

Principle #4: Good Requirements Demand Customer Involvement

No project is successful if the customer's expectations aren't met. Customer expectations can't be met if they aren't well understood, and only the customer can articulate his or her true expectations. The process of requirements discovery is not one that the requirements analyst can do alone. The requirements ultimately reside in the customer's mind. Discovering these clearly requires the customer's significant and ongoing involvement.

Recall that when the Standish Research Group asked IT executives to list the most important IT project success factors in their experience, the number one factor listed (given by 16 percent of the responding executives) was user involvement. In these executives' minds, the lack of user involvement was the number one factor leading to failed or challenged IT projects.

Principle #5: Requirements Are Never Perfect

Requirements discovery is a tedious iterative process. At some point, the requirements must be baselined so design can begin. The imprecise and difficult process of communication with users and customers makes it unlikely that the analysts can ever discover a complete and totally correct set of requirements. The discovery process we described can go on at some length and still not produce the perfect set of requirements.

So the requirements analyst must accept that there is always something forgotten or misunderstood, no matter how much time is devoted to discover the requirements. (Recall our analogy of the uncertainty principle from quantum physics with project requirements.) The appropriate strategy is to exert a best effort within the time the project allots and move on, accepting that some changes may be necessary as more is learned later. It is important for the project team to resist falling into analysis paralysis waiting for the perfect set of requirements to appear.

Knowing when to stop initial discovery and baseline the known requirements is one of the most difficult challenges for analysts and project managers. This can depend on the type of project and the perceived penalty of not getting the requirements "correct" at the outset. But the project team must accept that the requirements can never be perfect, and, at some point, the project must move forward with a set of baselined requirements that are further explored as the project unfolds.

Principle #6: Change in Requirements Is Inevitable

Because requirements are never perfect, the project team must plan for the inevitability of change as they and the customer discover new insights about the requirements. Hence it is vital to gain customer acceptance of a viable and reasonable change control process at the beginning of the project instead of making the unrealistic assumption that the requirements are finalized when baselined.

Knowing that it cannot articulate a complete and totally correct set of requirements at the beginning of the project, the project team should make sure that a commonly agreed on protocol for incorporating change in our projects is in place to accommodate additional requirements discoveries once the project work is underway. This change control process should allow a sensible consideration of newly discovered requirements, with a realistic cost/benefit analysis as the basis of whether additional requirements should be incorporated into the project. It is important that customers understand that incorporation of new requirements beyond those baselined generally involves increased cost and time.

Principle #7: Develop a Requirements Partnership

Because requirements are never perfect and change is inevitable, successful projects emerge from a partnership built on mutual trust and understanding between the project team and the customer. The team must do its part to establish and nurture this partnership by providing realistic estimates and commitments throughout the project and displaying flexibility when the inevitable changes occur. The customer must understand his or her role in establishing such a partnership as well.

Much of the conflict involved in projects arises from one or more of these seven principles for requirements. For example, customers do not fully understand that getting good requirements is a discovery process. They often think they have given the analysts perfectly good requirements from the beginning. In addition, they believe that there is a perfect set of requirements (the ones they have given, presumably), and are reluctant to accept the inevitability of change in requirements in projects. Thus, they often do not want to accept the increases in time or costs that these changes imply. In successful projects, customers and developers enter into a partnership, each party understanding and accepting the correct role of the other and the realities of software requirement discovery.

In summary, running IT as a business is the key to meeting the value challenge of fulfilling customer expectations relative to cost, time, and quality. Given the creative and open-ended nature of IT work coupled with the peculiar nature of software itself, the most difficult aspect of running IT as a business is maintaining a sharp focus on the underlying business goals. As we have discussed, this focus must be maintained at different levels within the organization. First, the organization must be careful at the strategic level to choose wisely from the many opportunities available, and this can be particularly daunting in IT with the rapid pace of technological change. However, the hedgehog concept can help the organization keep its strategic initiatives within its excellence zone, taking advantage of its expertise and its passion. The wise organization recognizes that efforts outside this zone are unlikely to succeed in the long term.

It is essential to establish a strategic focus for the entire organization. Once the proper strategic focus is attained, the organization must ensure it is maintained as the requisite work is organized and managed. Cultivating excellence in project management is one of the most important ways to do this. Without it, the creative forces acting in IT projects are likely to produce a dissipation of resources and energy and an accompanying deterioration in attaining cost and quality goals. Finally, but importantly, it is no accident that the IT roadway is littered with wrecked projects due to cost and schedule overruns driven by a poorly managed requirements discovery process. Hence at the technical level, requirements analysts must recognize the unusual nature of software requirements and focus sharply on the appropriate management of the IT requirements process.

Levels of Focus: An Example

The BlueCross BlueShield of South Carolina I/S Division has proactively established and maintained focus on the three levels we have discussed: strategic focus, project focus, and requirements focus.

The IT-OSD model was explicitly developed to provide an overall framework to guide the division's strategic thinking process. Ongoing scans of the external environment keep the organization abreast of trends and developments in both the client business environment and the IT industry. As a complement to this strategic thinking tool, the organization also articulated its hedgehog concept, which provides a sharper focus to its strategic goals and guides its commitment of resources to perceived opportunities.

More than a decade ago, I/S Division senior management realized that in order to accommodate a growing number of projects, a better and more focused approach was needed for managing projects. The division engaged Furman University's Institute for the Management of IT to assist in creating a comprehensive and systematic training program in project management concepts and principles tailored to the organization's own processes and culture.

The focal point of the training program is a project management certification program comprising eighteen days of training spread over an eight-month period. In the past ten years, almost three hundred participants have completed the program, with the majority of them also achieving the globally recognized certification by the Project Management Institute. The I/S Division has also created four project management offices within the overall organization that guide the practice and continued evolution of the project management discipline within the various units of the organization.

Encouraged by the demonstrated benefits of training and support for a more professional cadre of project leaders, the division also initiated an effort to produce a similar result for its systems analysts, who carry the major responsibility for discovering and articulating project requirements. The organization worked with Furman University to craft a customized systems analysis certification program, modeled after the successful project management program. Since 2004, almost five hundred participants have completed this program comprising seven days of training spread over a three-month period, and hundreds more have completed one or more stand-alone systems analysis classes.

These efforts show that the I/S Division works to maintain a sharp focus at the strategic, project, and requirements levels. These efforts have paid dividends; the organization has successfully managed a project work load that has increased dramatically since the late 1990s.

As we noted earlier, the successful IT organization must be run as a business, striking an appropriate balance between efficiency and effectiveness. In the book thus far we have explored the many characteristics of software development that make finding and maintaining this balance difficult. The efforts described here to establish and maintain multi-level focus are crucial components in accomplishing this balancing act. In the next chapter we explore another powerful component—the Hierarchical Matrix organization structure—that contributes to establishing and maintaining this balance.

Chapter 8

The Hierarchical Matrix Organization Model: Value and Scarcity

The trouble with organizing a thing is that pretty soon folks get to paying more attention to the organization than to what they're organized for.

Laura Ingalls Wilder

In the previous chapter, we discussed the importance of maintaining focus throughout the IT organization in order to run it as a successful business. Guided by the overall focus provided by the hedgehog concept, the organization must ensure that a corresponding and reinforcing focus is in place throughout. Achieving a proper expertise and focus in the discipline of project management and understanding the pivotal role that requirements management plays in IT are two central areas for this focus. However, achieving these two objectives—outstanding project management and the intelligent management of project requirements—produces the desired results only when coupled with effective and efficient management of resources.

Proper management of human resources implies careful attention to the organizational structure of the workforce. One major reason for this consideration is to balance the use of resources, which translate ultimately into cost for the customer, with the quality of the delivered products or services. The combination of cost and quality—the particular combination varies from customer to customer—defines value for customers. Of course, the ultimate goal is to deliver high quality products and services with as scarce a pool of resources as possible. The ideal is to operate as a resource-scarce organization but deliver the results of a resource-rich organization, producing maximum value for customers.

Clearly, the organization would like to adopt an organizational structure that increases the likelihood of achieving its strategic goals, which focus on creating customer value. The overall business mission and strategy is a major driver for the choice of organizational design. However, for an IT company, the system architecture places constraints and limitations on the mission and any implementation strategy adopted, and hence should be considered as well.

We must be sure that the architecture that exists supports the chosen mission/strategy. Otherwise, we must either choose a different mission/strategy or we must move the decision up one more level and ask if it is feasible to change the architecture. Of course the architecture *can be changed*, but making such a decision has long-reaching impact and implications, and should be undertaken only for compelling reasons. Even so, if the architecture and the mission/strategy are not mutually reinforcing, achieving the desired effectiveness and efficiency is difficult at best.

What we noted in chapter 5 about system architectures bears repeating here. It is not a matter of an IT organization choosing whether it will *have* a system architecture. Every operational IT organization has one. The critical issue is to invest the effort to articulate and understand its architecture and take an active approach to developing and maintaining it in ways that provide the strategic agility needed to address effectively its various clients' needs and business opportunities. Unless this is done, the organization's mission and related strategy are not optimally supported by the architecture, and it is unlikely that the best choices can be made about organizational structure.

Once a compatible and mutually reinforcing architecture and mission/strategy have been agreed on, the organization can begin to think about structure. As we see in later chapters, the organization's fundamental processes dictate the types of skills and specialties that it must possess and support. These skills and specialties drive the management hierarchy within the organization. However, for now we concentrate on the type of organization that might be chosen for the *IT workforce itself.*

We could express our underlying question: Which organizational workforce structure allows the organization to best use its system architecture in support of the company's primary obligation to provide value for clients by delivering excellent products and services in a cost-effective manner?

A Centralized or Decentralized Approach

A long-standing, persistent, high-level debate about IT organizational structure concerns the question of whether a centralized or decentralized approach would better serve an IT organization's purpose. As we will see, the debate continues because the answer to this depends on a variety of factors and there are pros and cons to both approaches.

A decentralized approach would involve dedicating IT resources to particular clients, customers, or lines of business. A natural consequence of this approach would be the opportunity of achieving a high degree of client responsiveness. If a subset of the workforce is dedicated to a single client, then those workers should develop a keen understanding of the client's business and its accompanying needs. Ideally, this depth of understanding would lead to the development of a level of expertise—both technical and business-related—that could result in the development of excellent products and services for the client. The decentralized approach, then, should deliver a high level of customer satisfaction with respect to the quality and appropriateness of products.

Further, the cohesiveness of work teams should be strengthened in the decentralized approach. Teams that develop expertise and have the opportunity to work together frequently are more likely to achieve and maintain a high level of performance. Such teams would be apt to spend less time understanding clients' issues and problems and more time focused on imagining effective solutions. Additionally, the requirements discovery partnership we outlined in the last chapter should be better achieved and nurtured in this approach, and hence the work teams should encounter fewer requirements issues downstream in projects.

On the other hand, the decentralized approach also has some potential disadvantages. It makes it more difficult to produce integration and synthesis across the IT organization. Teams know more about their clients' needs and tend to design solutions specifically focused on those needs; they are less inclined to look at similar needs across client boundaries and search for common solutions. The organization is less likely to identify and use synergies between applications in different client units.

This failure to recognize potential synergies is likely to produce duplication and wasted effort. Work teams may develop solutions specific to a client, when similar solutions have in fact already been produced for other clients. When teams working with different clients solve similar problems, the actual solutions may not be similar at all, because as we have seen, there are many degrees of freedom in designing solutions. The existence of different solutions to similar problems costs the organization in increased software maintenance and perhaps in duplicated, or at least redundant, hardware systems. For example, it is not uncommon in this situation to have a number of servers—each dedicated to a particular client's solutions—operating at suboptimum capacity. When this occurs, the organization is spending money for the housing, technical support, power consumption, and software licenses for servers that aren't actually needed.

As these considerations suggest, a distinct disadvantage of the decentralized approach is that it makes it harder to realize economy of scale in software development and maintenance as well as hardware procurement and maintenance. But yet another important disadvantage accrues from lack of workforce scale. Work groups in the decentralized approach tend to be smaller because they are scaled to particular clients' needs. While smaller work groups may be more cohesive, they are also less likely to develop the specialization that produces deep technical knowledge and expertise. This happens because the possible specializations cannot be justified economically.

Thus, the decentralized approach tends to result in a workforce consisting of generalists rather than specialists. This has a number of disadvantages. First, a lack of fully developed technical skills means that the quality of project work may suffer. Even if this potential deficiency is recognized, it may be necessary to supplement the project teams' work with contractors possessing the needed skill sets. Such workers typically are more expensive to the organization for two reasons. First, because they possess special skills, these workers command higher salaries; and second, as a general rule, contract workers are more expensive than regular workers per unit of work because they are employed on shorter terms through contracting agencies, which are paid additional fees.

In addition to the cost factor, the smaller work groups consisting of mostly generalists minimize the opportunity for team members to develop their skills at a deeper level. As generalists, they are engaged in a variety of tasks and have less time and a paucity of work assignments that would allow them the chance to extend their expertise and learn new techniques and technologies. Over time, this leads to a degradation of the general technical expertise level of the full-time staff and results in lower productivity. Eventually the impact extends to work teams' abilities to create the most current and effective solutions to clients' problems.

By contrast, a centralized organizational approach can reduce or even eliminate many of these disadvantages. More specifically, it allows for larger work groups and the opportunity for specialization. Group members have the opportunity to develop and expand technical skills, which leads to a more competent workforce in the long run. A centralized approach also enables the recognition and leveraging of synergies across various client boundaries, reducing duplication and wasted effort. Finally, it allows cost-effective use of infrastructure.

However, the centralized approach also introduces potentially negative issues that the decentralized approach minimizes. For example, in the centralized organization, work teams are likely formed dynamically in response to specific project needs. These *project teams* typically have less knowledge about the client's business environments needs, so they may be less effective in recognizing and solving client problems. Project teams in the centralized approach are also likely to be less cohesive since they are together for shorter periods. Further, in the centralized approach, resource allocations toward the needs and projects of particular clients are harder to manage, and no matter how this is done, it is likely to produce resource competition and tension among clients. Personal relationships with key client stakeholders become harder to develop and nurture, and the optimal client requirements partnerships are harder to create, lowering client satisfaction ratings.

As these considerations demonstrate, there is no single best answer as to whether to take a centralized or decentralized approach to organizational structure. The relative importance of the various factors we've identified differs from organization to organization, depending on its mission and basic competitive strategies. Just as importantly, the system architecture plays a central role. If an organization has a distributed system architecture, this makes it easier to consider adopting a decentralized approach—assuming the distributed architecture is aligned with the needs of various clients. On the other hand, if the organization employs a highly integrated system architecture, adopting a centralized organizational approach is more feasible, and more likely to support leveraging economies of scale than a decentralized approach. However, though it is an important consideration, the form of the architecture does not give a definitive answer to the question. Other factors such as client needs and expectations, fundamental competitive strategies, and the overall strategic goals of the organization must be factored in as well.

Some Common Types of Organizational Structure

Clearly, there are many ways to organize a group of individuals for a common purpose. In the myriad approaches to organizational structure that have been tried, three major categories have emerged as the most popular: the functional, the line of business, and the matrix. Not surprisingly, each of these structures has its strengths and weaknesses and the choice depends on an organization's overall mission and strategies.

Functional Organizational Structure

The functional organizational structure derives from a categorization of work that workers typically perform within an organization. Sometimes this categorization of work is specified in a departmental model, and within the departments, workers tend to perform a specific set of tasks. For example, workers in an accounting department are focused on the financial and accounting tasks of the business; those in an engineering department are tasked with the requisite engineering activities of the organization; those in marketing organize and implement the marketing strategies for the organization, and so on. Management controls in a functional organization are typically centralized as illustrated in figure 8.1.

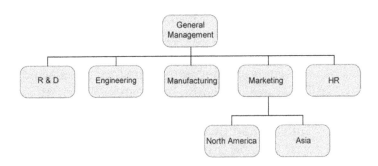

Figure 8.1: *Illustrating a Functional Organizational Structure.*

Functional work categories need not be limited to just top-level business activities but could also be extended to central operational tasks. For example, in an insurance company it may make sense to have specific and distinct workgroups devoted to group membership enrollment, individual membership enrollment, underwriting, claims adjustment, claims payment processing, customer service, and so on.

Thus, it may seem quite natural to adopt an organizational structure that allows such specialization of the organization's work. In a functional organizational structure, we would expect to accrue some distinct advantages. For example, the centralized coordination of activities in a functional structure makes producing a standardized line of products or services efficient and predictable. Indeed, each functional work group should achieve certain operational efficiencies in accomplishing its objectives. In addition, this structure allows the opportunity to develop a high level of expertise and applicable business intelligence within each work group.

However, this structure can also lead to a lack of communication among the functional groups within an organization, resulting in organizational silos, which make it difficult to recognize and react to changing market conditions. They can also contribute to inflexibility in other ways, making it difficult for customers to get problems and issues resolved.

Hence there are tradeoffs inherent in adopting a functional organizational structure. Some organizations might see more benefits than disadvantages to this structure, while others might experience just the opposite. For example, a functional organizational structure could be well suited for an organization that produces a highly standardized set of goods or services in large volume and at low cost. The efficiencies gained within the functional work groups help keep costs low and operational excellence high. Because the goods and services being produced are highly standardized, the ability to react quickly and flexibly to external conditions may not be a high priority. On the other hand, if the organization's market is more dynamic, efficiency and operational excellence may be less important than the ability to react to change quickly and surely. In this case the functional organizational structure may not be the best choice.

Line of Business Organizational Structure

The line of business organizational structure derives from a categorization of work at a higher level than that in the functional structure. In this structure, the work categories might typically be called divisions instead of departments (although there is no standard nomenclature). Each division within a line of business structure is actually a self-contained business. It may be focused on a single product or a group of related products, but in either case the division contains all the resources necessary for the design, construction, and marketing of the products for which it is responsible. For example, a vehicle manufacturing company might adopt a line of business structure with separate divisions for each of its major vehicle types, as illustrated in figure 8.2.

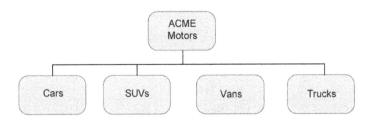

Figure 8.2: *Illustrating a Line of Business Organizational Structure.*

Another way divisions can be defined is on a geographical basis. So for example a company many have a North American division, an Asian division, and so on. These divisions are focused on producing and marketing their own set of products and services specifically designed for their region. Clearly an IT company could adopt the line of business approach based on either products or regions (or some combination of these).

As with the functional structure, the line of business structure has its advantages and disadvantages and its appropriateness depends on the organization's goals and strategies. Among its advantages is that it improves decision making within the divisions since decisions are taken with a focus on that division's business and not the total company perspective. By the same reasoning, it also fixes accountability more directly since each division is responsible solely for its own decisions and outcomes. Additionally, this organizational structure allows each division to organize and control all its own work, so coordination of the division's activities should be better.

On the other hand, the larger company loses opportunities for economies of scale that might be possible if resources and activities were spread across divisional boundaries. Additionally, this structure may foster competition between divisions. While some controlled competition is desirable, competition for the same markets and customers can prove damaging to the overall organization. Finally, it may be difficult to equitably allocate the costs of corporate-level staff, support, and overhead among divisions.

Matrix Organizational Structure

The matrix organizational structure brings together multifunctional teams to accomplish organizational objectives. These teams are typically assigned to projects or product development initiatives that require team members from different functional disciplines. These members are assigned to the work teams without removing them from their respective positions within the organization. They report on their day-to-day activities within the team to a project leader, but they continue to be evaluated on their overall performance by their manager within their designated department or functional group.

The matrix organization has a number of potential advantages. First, it provides the opportunity to produce superior solutions to satisfy client needs because the organization can bring together the specific resources required for excellent work on a given project. When managed properly, the matrix can also ensure efficient use of resources, assigning resources to work teams where skills and knowledge are most needed. In addition, it offers workers the opportunity to develop their technical expertise since they use their skills on a variety of projects over time. Further, the cross-pollination that multifunctional work teams produces can increase the coordination and integration across those units. The organization creates and develops a high level of project management expertise over time.

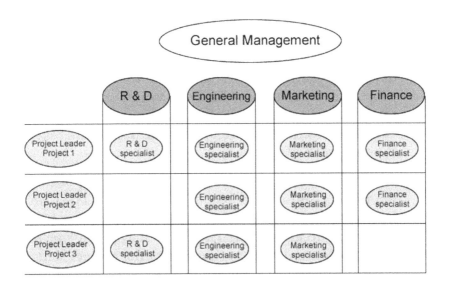

Figure 8.3: *Illustrating a Matrix Organizational Structure.*

However, a matrix organization necessitates new support mechanisms, organizational culture, and behavior patterns. Workers may feel conflicted as they report to both their functional manager and their project leaders. Further, in a matrix organization, there can be an inevitable conflict over resources and priorities as project teams vie for having the best resources available at the optimal time for their projects. These competing priorities and resource demands must be managed well for success. The competition for resources can also increase response times for clients as resources are distributed across a number of work teams. This structure increases organizational complexity, and care must be taken to avoid confusion and disagreements about accountability within the teams. Finally, without direct functional control, leaders must guard against the duplication of efforts among projects.

Within the matrix organizational model, there are three variants that can occur depending on how the actual projects are managed: the *weak matrix*, the *strong matrix*, and the *balanced matrix* structures.

- *Weak matrix:* A project coordinator or facilitator with limited authority is assigned to oversee the projects in this type of organization. The functional managers maintain day-to-day control over resources and usually have assigned project areas of responsibility as well. For these reasons, this type of matrix is sometimes referred to as a *functional matrix.* Accountability is clear in this structure and resources should not have the two-boss issue.

- *Strong matrix:* A project leader is primarily responsible for the project and is held accountable for its success. In this type of organization, functional managers provide and assign resources as needed, and they may provide technical expertise but only when requested by the project leader. Of the three matrix structures, this one is most common.

- *Balanced matrix:* A project leader is assigned to oversee projects, with power being shared equally between the project leader and the functional managers. Ideally, this could combine the best aspects of the weak and strong matrix structures. However, this is the most difficult structure to maintain, as the sharing of power is always tricky.

The Hierarchical Matrix: The Organizational Structure for IT

In the remainder of this chapter we introduce and discuss an adaptation of the matrix organizational structure called the Hierarchical Matrix. We believe that the Hierarchical Matrix structure offers some unique advantages to an IT organization as it blends some of the most desirable features of the functional and strong matrix approaches. This blended structure is particularly relevant to the challenge of balancing efficiency and effectiveness as it provides the IT organization the capabilities to operate efficiently with scarce resources, while maintaining the technical expertise and flexibility to deliver excellent products and services.

Work Division in the Hierarchical Matrix

In the Hierarchical Matrix organizational model, we make a clear distinction between the responsibilities of the technical workforce (the resources of the *matrix*) and management (the resources of the *hierarchy*). The key to ensuring the success of this approach is the creation of a framework of integrated highly developed, repeatable processes within both the matrix and the hierarchy.

Recall that the IT-OSD model summarizes the implementation of the IT organization's strategies as shown in figure 8.4. The diagram illustrates the fundamental purpose of organizational structure: to bring together resources and processes to accomplish the organization's work. By building the Hierarchical Matrix on the foundation of processes, this structure can be optimized for achieving this goal. Specifically, highly developed, repeatable processes and the framework these create allow people to focus on the particular responsibilities inherent in the organizational roles they are playing at any given time. In Laura Ingalls Wilder's phrase, this helps prevent folks from "paying more attention to the organization than to what they're organized for."

Figure 8.4: *Organizational Structure as an Enabler in the IT-OSD Model.*

Within the matrix, the technical workforce is responsible for effective problem solving and process management through the framework of highly repeatable *operational processes*. Members of the matrix have *total responsibility and accountability* for the success of the work to which they are assigned. The hierarchy, which is comprised of management, uses a framework of highly repeatable *administrative processes* to ensure the efficiency of the matrix. Members of the hierarchy are responsible for the following tasks.

- Set strategic direction and objectives for the company and procure work to meet those objectives.

- Acquire and maintain the technical infrastructure.

- Acquire, evaluate, mentor, and nurture the people who make up the technical workforce.

- Provide training and development opportunities as needed.

In essence, it is the job of the workforce to provide the technical competence to ensure the effective and timely completion of excellent work, while management is responsible for ensuring the quality of the infrastructure and the workforce and using them efficiently to achieve the company's strategic objectives.

Work is completed within the matrix, which operates under the *strong matrix* model. Teams are assembled dynamically according to the work to be completed, and it is normal for many of the matrix resources to be working on multiple efforts at one time. This leads to a substantial level of complexity within which appropriate resources must be assigned and scheduled in advance. It can also make the management of individual work efforts challenging, as resources are often pulled in multiple directions at once. The fact that the matrix is built on a foundation of well-defined processes can help offset much of this potential complexity and conflict.

Specialization and Interdependence in the Hierarchical Matrix

The design of the Hierarchical Matrix is driven by a number of fundamental assumptions or tenets reflecting both overall strategy and human nature. At the high level, this matrix is based on a specialization strategy centered on basic IT processes, which leads to an effective workforce with increased technical competence. This specialization strategy makes it easier to attract and retain the best technical talent by offering more challenging work, supportive and invigorating peer work groups, and more opportunities to develop and expand technical skills. (We explore this specialization strategy in chapter 10.) Now we want to focus on the impact that specialization has on the underlying design of the Hierarchical Matrix.

Assuming a strategy to allow people to specialize, the Hierarchical Matrix structure recognizes that the more people specialize, the more interdependent they become. To give an analogy, a hundred and fifty years ago when most people in the United States lived on large family farms, there was little opportunity to specialize work. These farms were essentially self-contained except for the occasional product like coffee, sugar, and lamp oil. Most of the family's food was grown on the farm, their clothes were made there, wood was cut from trees on the farm for heat and construction, heavy labor was provided by the farm animals whose food was also raised on the farm, and so on. Everyone had to acquire a variety of skills for the comfort, and even survival, of the group. By the nature of this situation, interdependence on others outside the farm was minimized.

By contrast, with the specialization that now characterizes our economy, few of us would be able to survive without a host of products and services provided by others. The specialization supported by the Hierarchical Matrix model produces the same kinds of interdependence. The work products that are one person's output are another person's input on the same work effort. Some of the specialized activities that a work effort requires likely come from a number of different people, some of whom may only be on the team for a short while.

Toward the goal of productively managing such interdependence, the matrix is designed around a *framework of highly developed, repeatable administrative and operational processes* through which people come together for effective problem solving and process management. The resources needed for success must be brought to bear on the problems at hand, regardless of where they are positioned within the hierarchy or the matrix. Importantly, the matrix is designed so that no interaction with the hierarchy is required for it to operate successfully in the vast majority of situations.

As a consequence, to achieve a successful outcome, team members must know how to seek out and acquire the help needed from others, and they must accept the responsibility to do this. Each repeatable process within the matrix is designed to provide the freedom for each person to act by showing them how the various technical roles interrelate and by identifying the responsibility for each person to get the help they need from others to be successful. Assumed acceptance of this dual reality—the responsibility to get help and the freedom to do so—is at the heart of the matrix.

So a basic underlying tenet is that the more people specialize, the more they require a framework that provides definitions of highly developed, repeatable processes to accomplish the desired outcomes. This framework also improves day-to-day decisions by ensuring that each repeatable process within the matrix contains an independent decision-making process based on collaboration and consensus that includes checks and balances and escalation procedures.

Conflict and Escalation in the Hierarchical Matrix

The existence of checks and balances within the matrix framework is one of its essential features. In order for the matrix to function well with minimal intervention by the hierarchy, problem resolution must be enabled to occur naturally. This brings us to a fundamental concept, and one that goes in the face of human nature. In the Hierarchical Matrix model, *conflict and escalation must not be viewed as negative outcomes.* If this happens and escalation is not used when it should be, a serious outcome results—the matrix work is simply not accomplished successfully. The reason for this is that conflict and escalation are *planned success strategies* for the Hierarchical Matrix.

For example, it is not uncommon for conflicts over available resources to arise in the day-to-day matrix work. Project leaders should always make the assumption that the projects they are leading have a top organizational priority. Prioritization of projects is not an issue that project leaders should worry about or try to resolve; in fact prioritization is not an issue that *can be* resolved at the project level. Rather, project leaders should be sharply focused on one thing: bringing their projects to a successful conclusion on time and within budget.

When resource availability interferes with this goal on a project, it becomes the project leader's job to facilitate the resolution of this issue. Sometimes, an accommodation can be worked out within the team itself. Perhaps the work can be shifted; perhaps someone can work overtime; perhaps the project schedule can be reworked to accommodate, and so on. If the issue cannot be resolved within the team, the project leader should consult with leaders of other projects to see if it might be possible to do some resource shifting among teams to manage the issue. If this fails, the project leader should bring the resource issue to the attention of the appropriate first-line functional manager—that is, the functional manager that directly controls the type of resource needed.

If the project leader has employed effective planning techniques, this request should come with enough lead time for the functional manager to accommodate the request by either rearranging work schedules for his/her resources, or by obtaining a new resource from a contractor pool. Effective planning allows the majority of resource conflicts to be solved in one of these three basic ways: resolution of the conflict within the project team, accommodation among project leaders, or obtaining the needed resource from the applicable first-line functional manager.

However, if for whatever reasons, the resource request comes to the functional manager with a short deadline, the manager may determine that it is not possible to respond favorably to the resource request. In this case, the project leader has two options: (1) accept the fact that no resource is currently available and adjust the project schedule accordingly, or (2) escalate the request to the next higher level in the hierarchy. The project leader should consider the first of these two options to be feasible only if the project schedule has enough float to accommodate a delay for the needed resource.

If accepting the current lack of a needed resource pushes the project schedule out, the project leader is going to have to answer to stakeholders about this delay. Clearly this is not a good outcome for the project leader, but worse yet, this may be a bad outcome for the organization. For example, other projects (perhaps unknown to the project leader) may be dependent on this particular project finishing on schedule. Or pushing this project's schedule may obligate additional resources during periods when they are already fully scheduled. A project leader's primary job and focus is on bringing projects in on time and on budget; everything else should be secondary. So rather than accepting this situation, the project leader's next step should ordinarily be to consider an escalation of the issue through the proper chain of command within the hierarchy.

Escalation is a powerful tool for resolving issues that the project leader (or others) cannot resolve locally. It should be used to ensure the timely resolution of issues and decisions, assign accountability for resolution, and aid in identifying mitigation actions. Human nature enters the picture because the need for escalation arises out of conflict, and most people prefer to avoid conflict if possible. Indeed, we are taught from a young age that failure to resolve conflict is usually a bad reflection on us as individuals. But what is important to understand about resource conflict in the Hierarchical Matrix—which we refer to as *focused conflict*—is that it is not only inevitable, but it's necessary and healthy for the organization. Focused conflict over resources is built into the Hierarchical Matrix design. It is the alert mechanism that leads to the tweaking required to maintain the proper balance of Hierarchical Matrix work flow.

Escalation as Collaborative Negotiation

For escalation to function properly as a Hierarchical Matrix success strategy, it should be viewed as a collaborative form of negotiation. We have already emphasized that escalation and the conflict that leads to it must not be viewed as negative outcomes within the Hierarchical Matrix model. Adopting the viewpoint of escalation as collaborative negotiation helps emphasize this perspective. Negotiation within the collaborative context of the Hierarchical Matrix can be defined as a process by which two or more parties search for a resolution that promotes their common interest in the success of the organization.

In order for escalation to become a collaborative negotiation as opposed to an unpleasant confrontation, those in the organization must understand the underlying principles of proper escalation. The most fundamental of these principles is that escalation is not seen as failure on the part of the escalator or the individual to which the escalation is taken. It is rather an essential tool in ensuring that issues that cannot be resolved by an individual are elevated to the next organizational level.

Collaborative negotiations should be conducted diplomatically but nonetheless firmly. Escalation should always be about a project issue, never about personalities. An escalation is never viewed as being done "on a person" but is rather done on an unresolved issue. To be effective, escalations should be done in a timely manner, meaning that they should be initiated in time for the person to whom the issue is being escalated to affect a proper resolution before negative consequences prevail for the project. Except in emergency situations, communication should take place prior to an escalation, signaling that there is a risk or issue being managed that might require an escalation to resolve. The goal is a "no surprises" approach, which helps maintain the collaborative nature of the escalation resolution process.

While all project team members are empowered to escalate, there are also certain common sense protocols that should be observed before an escalation is initiated. For example, the issues at hand should first be discussed within the team so that the team can search for its own resolution. If a resolution still isn't possible, team members are then aware of and supportive of the escalation.

Once initiated, an escalation must be managed. It is usually not sufficient to simply escalate; the escalator must continue to monitor the situation and track the progress of the resolution. An important part of escalation management is to properly document the escalation. Verbal escalation may be the method of choice, especially if there is a time critical nature to the escalation, but this should always be followed up with written or email documentation. This documentation should include the issue at hand, the escalation action, the name of the individual escalating the issue, the person to whom the escalation is taken, the required outcome, the critical timeframe, and the consequences to the project effort if the issue is not resolved. This documentation helps avoid confusion about the source, rationale and the intent of the escalation. If a resolution is not obtained in a timely manner, another escalation may be required.

A final observation about collaborative negotiations: they should be conducted as amicably and efficiently as possible, with the emphasis always on finding the resolution that best serves the goals and objectives of the organization. Conflict that arises from personality or personal issues among workers is not part of the planned success strategies for the matrix, nor is it part of the focused conflict that is inherent in the matrix. It should be dealt with as directly as possible, invoking the help of the hierarchy when needed. Recall that the hierarchy is responsible for ensuring the quality of the workforce and its efficiency in achieving the strategic objectives of the company. Clearly, helping to resolve personal conflicts within the technical workforce falls within the scope of this responsibility.

The Self-Correcting Nature of the Hierarchical Matrix

We mentioned earlier that within the Hierarchical Matrix structure, the matrix is designed to resolve most issues without intervention from the hierarchy. The key to this is that the matrix contains its own check-and-balance mechanisms that make it a largely self-correcting entity that can maintain a near-optimal use of technical resources.

With a total matrix workload comprising many efforts, the hierarchy (management) cannot be clever enough or well enough informed to plan and maintain a work flow that optimizes the use of all available resources at any given time. Indeed, if the control of work flow and resource scheduling in the matrix were left entirely in the hands of management, two things would happen. First the organization would need a large number of managers to attempt to implement the intricate scheduling and planning that would be required to accomplish this. And second, no matter how diligently this large cadre of managers worked at this task, they would ultimately fail.

This outcome is driven by the unpredictable course of software development projects. We have earlier considered the unusual nature of software itself as a product. We have also seen the inherent and unavoidable challenges in discovering and articulating complete requirements for software projects and the rework and schedule delays this often produces. And finally, we have explored the fact that software development is at its heart a creative endeavor with all the uncertainties that this implies.

All of these factors contribute significantly to the fundamental unpredictability of the software development process. No sooner does a software development project get underway than do unexpected delays and difficulties arise. When you consider the immense challenge of tackling a large number of such projects concurrently, all of which draw resources from a common pool of workers specializing in a variety of subprocesses, the prospect of using resources efficiently is daunting! No management team could hope to plan and manage this in an optimal way on its own.

The beauty and great advantage of the Hierarchical Matrix structure is that management does not have this task. The matrix, with its repeatable processes and the use of focused conflict and escalation, can manage most of this on its own. A simple metaphor might help illustrate the basic roles of focused conflict and escalation. Consider the operation of a kitchen pressure cooker. We can think of conflict as the steam inside the pressure cooker. For the cooker to do its job, steam must be present. However, if we overheat the cooker and let the steam build up to excess, the entire cooker could explode. To prevent this, pressure cookers come equipped with steam release valves.

The valve represents the role of escalation. When properly set, the release valve addresses and resolves the issue of the building pressure of the steam. On the other hand, if the pressure release valve is set too low, the cooker releases too much steam and does not function properly—just as too much escalation destroys the effectiveness of the matrix. Of course, if the pressure release valve is set too high, the result is even worse—just as the reluctance or refusal to use escalation can bring serious consequences to the matrix.

Put another way, focused conflict over resources provides an essential alert system to draw attention to projects in the matrix that need some sort of intervention. If this focused conflict is well understood, employed as a strategy, and not treated as an unfortunate and unwanted distraction, in most cases the required intervention can be handled within the matrix with the routine involvement of frontline functional managers.

As our earlier resource conflict discussion illustrated, project leaders should take the lead in resolving resource allocation issues as near to the project level as possible. This is why a focus on project management excellence is so important for the organization. On those occasions when it becomes necessary, escalation should be used to bring the required project intervention to the attention of the appropriate level of the hierarchy. If conducted properly, escalations reach senior management only in rare cases.

The role of the hierarchy within the escalation strategy is to remove obstacles that are hindering the successful completion of projects. This may involve supplying additional resources in some cases, or in other cases rearranging project priorities. Recall that project leaders should never be concerned with project priorities—all their projects are a top priority as far as they are concerned. The truth is that project leaders do not have the sufficient organizational perspective or overview to make accurate priority determinations. So when a priority decision is required—for example, when there simply aren't enough resources of one or more types to go around at the moment—the hierarchy must provide this perspective and make such prioritization decisions.

On rare occasions, an escalation can expose a more systemic issue or problem within the organization. When this occurs, the escalation helps the hierarchy recognize the need for different kinds of adjustments and decisions. For most issues, the Hierarchical Matrix processes already have in place the decision-making mechanism to reach a resolution. But in some cases, gaps or flaws in these processes and their inherent decision-making mechanisms might be discovered. When this occurs, *metadecisions*—or decisions about the processes and decision-making structure—are called for. In these cases, the conflict and escalation strategies call to the organization's attention the need for metadecisions—yet another way the Hierarchical Matrix is able to engage in a process of self-correction.

Balancing Efficiency and Effectiveness

In the previous chapter we considered how overcoming the challenge of maintaining proper focus at multiple levels can contribute to the successful running of IT as a business. In this chapter we have explored an approach to surmounting the second major challenge in running IT as a business, namely the balancing of efficiency and effectiveness. Putting it another way, the purpose of the Hierarchical Matrix is to allow the IT business to operate as a resource-scarce organization (efficiency), but produce solutions for its clients as if it were resource-rich (effectiveness). The beauty of the Hierarchical Matrix is that its self-correcting mechanisms allow it to find equilibrium naturally in most cases, thus obtaining an appropriate balance between these two critical characteristics.

Another metaphor illustrates the intent of this self-correcting design. Think of the matrix as an automobile engine. The purpose of the engine is to provide the power to propel an automobile down the road. Let's assume we are driving on a stretch of expressway with little traffic, and we put the car on cruise control. The engine is now working ideally; it literally hums along with an optimal mix of power (effectiveness) and efficiency. Of course road conditions are not constant. The automobile inevitably encounters obstacles—rough surfaces, hills of varying degrees of steepness, and so on. When this happens, the cruise control mechanism recognizes the need for more or less power and supplies it without intervention from the driver (the hierarchy).

Of course, on occasion some driver intervention may be required to switch lanes, tap the brake, or press the accelerator, but the engine and its cruise control mechanism can handle the bulk of the tasks (remember we assumed little traffic). On much rarer occasions, the engine may sputter, indicating the possibility of a serious problem. In these cases the driver must pull over and attend to the problem—a repair or some engine adjustments (a metadecision) may be called for.

The Hierarchical Matrix: An Example

For more than twenty years, BlueCross BlueShield of South Carolina has operated its insurance business as a line-of-business organization. As a consequence, the bulk of activities and business functions are decentralized; each line of business is responsible for its own products, services, marketing, sales, and customer satisfaction. However, within this structure, two major areas have been purposely reserved at the corporate level as centralized functions: finance and information technology. The specific reasons for centralizing these functions differ, but for IT, a primary consideration is the cost effectiveness that can be realized through economies of scale and scope. Essentially all IT work is organized and performed within the company's I/S Division, with the CIO reporting directly to the CEO of the company.

Hence, the I/S Division operates as a centralized *business-within-a-business* in the context of an overall decentralized line-of-business company. Within this structure, the division is committed to realizing the economies of scope and scale that are the primary drivers for its centralized position. Indeed, the I/S hedgehog concept that we discussed in the previous chapter reflects this perspective, especially in the stated objective of the division to *become the best in the world at combining people and technology to produce low-cost healthcare payer back-office processing.*

Since the early 1990s, the division has used an evolutionary approach to develop the Hierarchical Matrix as its basic organizational design. Of course the proof of the value and quality of any design is whether it actually works. And that is the true beauty of the Hierarchical Matrix—*it does work.* In fact, it is one of the major success factors that has enabled the division to maintain the proper balance between efficiency and effectiveness to become an industry leader in providing low-cost, high-quality healthcare payer back-office processing.

Chapter 9

Defining the Hierarchical Matrix Model: Nine Fundamental IT Processes

If you can't describe what you are doing as a process, you don't know what you're doing.

W. Edwards Deming

As we saw in the previous chapter, the Hierarchical Matrix organizational structure has the potential to enable the effective and efficient management of resources in an IT organization, allowing the organization to maintain both the technical expertise and the flexibility to deliver excellent products and services at reasonable costs to its clients. However, the inherent complexity of this organizational structure also presents some unique management challenges.

The key to meeting these challenges lies in the underlying design of the matrix and its connections to the hierarchy. As we saw, ideally the matrix should embody its own check-and-balance mechanisms, making it a largely self-correcting entity that can maintain a near-optimal use of technical resources without continual intervention from the hierarchy. The success of this approach depends explicitly on a framework of integrated highly developed, repeatable processes within the matrix and a metadecision process within the hierarchy used to investigate why an issue could not be resolved within the matrix. Properly defined and managed, these processes and the framework they embody allow people to focus on the particular responsibilities inherent in the roles they are playing within the work of the organization at any given time.

Defining the Fundamental IT Processes

How then should we go about defining the appropriate Hierarchical Matrix processes? This is a complex issue, and resolving it requires a careful analysis of the IT organization's work as well as IT industry best practices. As with much of our analysis, a good starting point is the IT-OSD model.

Recall that in the IT-OSD model the fundamental purpose of organizational structure is to bring together resources and processes to accomplish the organization's work. There are three basic types of IT resources: application systems, infrastructure on which these systems run, and the people required to build and maintain both of these and to deliver the end result. Hence we must ensure that appropriate processes are in place for managing application systems, infrastructure, and people.

In any IT organization, processes dealing with these three resources are surely present. However, the presence of a certain number of processes intended to manage and enable these resources does not guarantee success. The key factors for creating processes that can drive the organization's success are contained in the phrase we used above, namely: "a framework of integrated highly developed, repeatable processes." Looking at the various components of this phrase helps illustrate its true meaning and power.

First, the set of processes collectively define a *framework* for the organization's work. A truly useful and effective framework must encompass *all the work necessary* for the successful delivery of excellent products and services to clients. The framework provides the total context of the organization's work and guides the individuals doing the work through the various stages required for success. To be effective in this sense, the framework must be complete—that is, it must encompass all necessary work. There must be no missing processes within the framework.

The framework must contain *highly developed* processes. This means that the chosen processes must not only be complete when taken together, but each process must also provide sufficient guidance for the work within its scope. Note that this does not imply that the processes specify or dictate all the work to be done in minute detail. Indeed, it is a basic premise of this book that the IT profession demands a high level of creativity; the processes must respect the inherent flexibility and degrees of freedom that this premise implies. What highly developed means in this context is that all processes provide guidelines that are flexible enough to allow sufficient creativity yet developed thoroughly enough to provide guidance and basic principles that provide the thoughtful professional with appropriate boundaries for the exercise of the required creativity.

Another way to express this is to say that a central feature of being highly developed is that each process must contain its own internal decision-making procedures. We have noted that the key to the success of the Hierarchical Matrix model is that the matrix must act as a largely *self-correcting entity*, requiring as little intervention from the hierarchy as possible. To accomplish this, those working in the matrix must understand and accept the freedom and responsibility to make decisions and act on them. Hence the presence within the various processes of well-defined internal decision-making procedures is absolutely essential. Our discussion in the previous chapter of how resource allocation issues are most often resolved by project leaders with little or no involvement of the hierarchy illustrates this point. This can occur because the project management processes have built-in decision-making procedures and norms that are well understood by project leaders as well as others in the matrix.

A concept closely related to being well developed is that all processes must also be *repeatable*. This means that even though creativity is allowed, the process results must be predictable. In other words, if two IT professionals use a given process in similar situations, they should arrive at comparable and compatible end points. This requirement is absolutely necessary to avoid the chaos that would prevail if unrestrained creativity were allowed to rule the day.

Finally, repeatable processes allow the design of a *set of processes* that are tightly *integrated*. This means that the processes work together smoothly to produce a given result. As a good example of this, consider again the resolution of the resource allocation issue discussed earlier. We noted that the project management processes have built-in decision-making procedures that lead to a resolution of such issues in the large majority of cases. However, when this process fails to produce a resolution, the process of escalation is invoked. Escalation is another of the highly developed, repeatable processes and hence has its own internal decision-making procedures. These procedures allow the vast majority of escalations to resolve the relevant issue.

As stated earlier, in those relatively rare cases where no resolution can be agreed on after escalation within the matrix, a metadecision process within the hierarchy investigates why the issue was not resolved. The metadecision process has its own decision-making procedures that question whether the processes need some adjustment or whether the difficulties lie in misunderstandings of those processes by those involved. The point is that all these processes are tightly integrated so that the hand off from one process to another is done smoothly and naturally. The predictable repeatability of the processes makes this possible, and the understanding of the various process interfaces reduces stress and conflict within the matrix while enhancing problem and issue resolution.

Figure 9.1: *Modeling the set of processes as meshed gears.*

As an analogy of this total process framework, consider figure 9.1, which models the set of processes as a set of gears of different sizes that are meshed together to accomplish a predictable end result inside a traditional (i.e., non-digital) timepiece. If these gears are to accomplish the desired result, they must be a complete *framework*—one missing gear ruins the result. Further, each gear must be *highly developed*—a missing or partially completed gear tooth leads to unpredictable or failed results. And if the gears do not operate in a *repeatable* manner—if one or more wobbles or turns at an unpredictable rate, for example—we again fail to achieve the intended results. Finally, if the gears are not correctly *integrated*—that is, if they are not properly meshed—the entire mechanism jams up and will not work at all. On the other hand, if all the necessary gears are formed and set correctly, we get a complete framework of integrated, highly developed, repeatable gears—the fine timepiece we hoped for, that operates beautifully with only the occasional intervention for winding or cleaning.

Within this context, let us return to the task of defining the framework of a highly integrated and scalable set of administrative and operational processes for an IT organization. An important strategy to use in defining such a framework is the appropriate *adaptation* of selected IT industry best-practice frameworks for various elements of an organization's administration and operations. It is important to remember that all industry best-practice frameworks are independent, have overlapping components, and have strengths and weaknesses. This is why the adaptation process is so important.

The following best-practice frameworks are used in our adaptation process:

- The **Information Technology Infrastructure Library** (ITIL) is a framework of internationally defined best practices for IT service management and support developed by the government of the United Kingdom and published by the IT Service Management Forum. This is a comprehensive IT framework that focuses on IT service and infrastructure, management.

- The **Capability Maturity Model Integration** (CMMI), developed by the Software Engineering Institute, is a model for process improvement described in terms of best practices within a framework. This framework focuses on IT project management and application software engineering.

- **Control Objectives for Information and related Technology (COBIT)** is an open standard and framework of controls and best practices for IT governance. It is published by ITGI, a not-for-profit research organization affiliated with the Information Systems Audit and Control Association. This framework focuses on IT governance and management controls.

- The **Enterprise Architecture Maturity Model (EAMM),** developed by the National Association of State Chief Information Officers, is a model for systems architecture process improvement.

At a high level, we can think of the processes as belonging to one of three categories. One category concerns optimizing organizational change and monitoring and controlling the other processes to ensure the overall quality necessary for the long-term success of the organization. We refer to this category as the *adaptive change* process group. A second category focuses on building and maintaining the necessary client relationships and ensuring the effectiveness of supporting basic business functions such as planning and budgeting, financial and cost accounting, resource acquisition, contract management, and marketing. We refer to this category as the *business perspective* process group. The third category comprises the set of processes that manage the production of products and services for the organization's clients. We will refer to this category as the *system factory* process group.

Guided by the best-practice frameworks for various aspects of the IT industry referenced above, we have identified a total of nine processes that are distributed among these three process group categories. Each of these processes can be further refined into subprocesses that adapt to particular needs, but we believe that these nine encapsulate a complete framework for any IT organization.

The Adaptive Change Process Group

Recall from chapter 2 our discussion of the advantages of evolutionary rather than revolutionary change—a process we referred to as adaptive change. Constructive adaptive change results from a mentality of continuous improvement. It depends on a willingness to change and modify existing products, services, and processes more than it depends on creating completely new directions. In short, its successful application depends on using critical assessments of the present to help create the future—which sums up the purpose of the adaptive change process group.

This process group contains one major process, the *adaptive change management* process. Within this process, we identify two integrated subprocesses—an *IT governance* subprocess and a *quality assurance* subprocess. IT governance should provide for the orderly consideration of change in the technologies, technical methods, processes, and procedures of the organization as well as organizational policies and management practices. Ideally, IT governance allows employees the opportunity to supply input and engage in meaningful participation in the adaptive change management process. If defined and managed well, IT governance can encourage a culture of innovation.

Quality assurance complements and supports IT governance. Any suggested changes must be evaluated and analyzed before any actions can be taken on them. The quality assurance subprocess can help provide appropriate evaluation about the current state and performance of the organization, which can inform analysis. In addition, quality assurance can uncover areas for improvement. Once these areas for improvement have been analyzed, proposed change and adaptation can be inserted into the IT governance system. The adaptive change process, therefore, comprises the IT governance and quality assurance subprocesses, which work together to fuel innovation and evolutionary change.

The Business Perspective Process Group

The purpose of the business perspective process group is the financial management of an IT company or an internal IT organization as well as the overall management of client relationships within two major processes: *line of business management* and *client management*.

LOB Management

The line of business (LOB) management process is focused primarily on ensuring that the IT organization's products and services are provided in a cost-effective manner to its clients. The scope of cost management in this context includes the use of the three major IT resources of application systems, infrastructure, and people. Within the LOB management process, subprocesses are needed to promote the wise and cost-effective use of IT resources in the pursuit of client business goals. Such subprocesses include the establishment and performance of a cost accounting and tracking system that provides an accurate allocation of costs to the various clients. In addition, subprocesses are needed to ensure cost-effective resource acquisition and contract management.

Client Management

In chapter 4, we identified some of the mutual advantages that the IT organization and its clients can realize from the building of strategic client relationships. We also described the importance of the concept of enabling client focus in building these relationships. The client focus approach allows the client organization to focus on what it knows best—succeeding in its own business environment—while permitting the IT organization to focus on its expertise in providing outstanding IT solutions that are appropriate and cost-effective for the client's business needs.

The success of the client focus approach depends on the development of mutual trust in the client relationship. The client management process is focused on achieving this trust. In support of this larger goal, subprocesses are needed to ensure appropriate communication and coordination with clients at strategic, tactical, and operational levels.

The System Factory Process Group

The purpose of the system factory process group is the creating, maintaining, executing, and hosting of self-created systems, as well as the selecting, installing, executing and hosting of vendor-supplied systems, or some combination of these two approaches, in support of the specific requirements of a given client.

We identify six major processes within the system factory process group. The first of these recognizes the central importance of the system architecture and is called *system architecture management*. The second major process deals with *application systems management*. This central process involves the creation or acquisition, implementation, support, and management of application systems to manage the data processing and process automation required to run a client's business efficiently and effectively.

Further, to accomplish excellent IT service management and support, we identify three additional major processes within the system factory process group: *service management, information and communications technology (ICT) infrastructure management*, and *security and audit management*. Finally, the sixth major process within the system factory category is a collection of subprocesses included in *enabling support management.* Its constituent subprocesses are focused on the acquisition of and caring for the people in the organization as well as the administrative tasks needed to ensure the smooth operation of the other process groups within the system factory process group category.

The following are brief descriptions the six major processes within the system factory process group.

System Architecture Management

Recall that the system architecture defines the capabilities required to produce IT products and services that meet clients' business needs, describes how these products and services are to be organized and provided, specifies what IT resources they require, and identifies what common product and service components can be leveraged across the needs of multiple clients.

Note that a key consequence of the interconnection of the system architecture and the business needs of clients is that the architecture must be dynamic because it must change as the inevitable changes in client business needs evolve. However, because the system architecture determines and provides the fundamental capabilities of the IT organization, it should change slowly and deliberately.

Clearly, deliberate change requires careful management. Recall that one of the greatest challenges facing an IT organization is to ensure the conceptual integrity of its underlying architecture. Certainly, design considerations are paramount in managing the architecture. The goal is ensure that the underlying design emanates, or at least that it appears to emanate, from one mind or a small group of agreeing minds. It is difficult to maintain such conceptual integrity over time as infrastructure is updated and as large system products are modified and extended by those who had no involvement in the original design and development effort. This can be accomplished only by excellent management control processes to ensure that new components are designed within appropriate constraints.

Application Systems Management

The primary organizing principle for an effective application system management process is the product development life-cycle model, which defines the product development approach used to administer all aspects of requirements definition, design, and building or procurement of a solution based on these requirements. This includes a system development methodology that specifies more particularly within the overall product life-cycle model the various methods to be used and how they interrelate. An appropriate project management subprocess should be in place to provide an umbrella set of techniques and methods to manage the development project—stakeholder communications, planning, budget, and schedule—as distinguished from managing the actual product development work itself, which is guided by the methods and techniques defined within the system development methodology. Finally, subprocesses must be present for ongoing support and monitoring of the developed solutions.

Service Management

Great service is at the heart of a successful IT business, as it is for most businesses. Indeed, the ideal steady-state situation consists of users effectively employing an application system provided by the technical infrastructure to optimize their own work. The client focus we discussed earlier has this very situation as its goal: system users focused on their own work, which is being enabled and empowered by the all but transparent products and services provided by the IT organization. As a consequence, service management is an important process group for the organization.

The service management process can be broken into two complementary subprocesses that enable the *delivery* of great service and effective service *support* that ensure the client's ongoing satisfaction with the delivered service. Service support is typically initiated with a routing process that effectively routes service requests and incident reports to the appropriate additional subprocesses, including problem management, change management, configuration management, and release management. Of course, subprocesses should also be in place to provide timely feedback to users on the resolution of their submitted service requests or incidents.

ICT Infrastructure Management

Great service requires a robust, reliable, and capable technical infrastructure. Hence an ICT infrastructure management process must be present to effectively manage the infrastructure. This process should include subprocesses to ensure effective ICT deployment, management of operations, and delivery of technical support. Further, a project management subprocess ensures that infrastructure development and maintenance work is effectively planned, implemented, and smoothly integrated with other processes when needed.

Security and Audit Management

Security and audit management processes operate continuously across the organization to control the provision of information, to prevent its unauthorized use, and to provide support for audits of the IT organization by internal and external entities. One of the subprocesses is security management, which defines the needed level of security taking into consideration internal requirements as well as meeting the security requirements specified in service level agreements (SLAs) and external contractual or legal requirements. The second subprocess is audit management, which insures that the response required to an audit is accurate and timely and that any audit findings are responded to appropriately.

Enabling Support Management

The enabling support management processes comprise two main subprocesses that are concerned with the people in the organization as well as the administrative tasks needed to ensure the smooth operation of the other processes. This includes provisions for such tasks as screening prospective employees, evaluating performance, career path advising, mentoring and coaching, providing appropriate training opportunities, team building, assigning resources to project teams, and resolving conflicts.

The IT Organization Process Framework

The nine fundamental processes described here form what we believe to be a complete process framework for an IT organization. Additional processes can be derived by refining these processes into finer granularity based on changing conditions and new insights, while remembering this granularity should reflect the specific mission, goals and objectives, and driving strategies of a given IT organization. We suggest a first-level refinement, summarized in table 9.1, of these nine fundamental processes that may well apply to most IT organizations.

Applying the Process Framework: An Example

The identification and refinement of the nine fundamental IT processes has been an evolutionary process within the I/S Division of BlueCross BlueShield of South Carolina. Indeed, the refinement of these processes is an ongoing task driven by changes in technology, best practices in the IT industry, the client business environment, and emerging understanding of and insights into what works best for the organization. Whenever an existing subprocess is found deficient in some way, it is modified or calibrated to match changing conditions as the needs dictate. On occasion, needs for new subprocesses emerge, and these are added as these needs are recognized and validated. Within the stable process framework, the refined subprocess structure is dynamic, and it is modified and developed with changing conditions and new insights.

Table 9.1

Summary of Fundamental IT Processes

IT Process Framework

Adaptive Change — 1. **Adaptive Change Management**
   - IT governance
   - Quality assurance

2. **Line of Business Management**

Business Perspective
   - Financial management
   - Resource acquisition
   - Planning

3. **Client Management**
   - Relationship management
   - Steering support (client work requests)
   - Product improvement
   - Systems/service monitoring
   - Internal marketing

4. **System Architecture Management**
   - Application system architecture
   - Infrastructure architecture

5. **Application Systems Management**
   - Product development life cycle
   - Project management
   - Ongoing support and monitoring

6. **Service Management**

System Factory
   - Service support
   - Service delivery

7. **ICT Infrastructure Management**
   - Project management
   - Infrastructure deployment management
   - Operations management
   - Technical support

8. **Security and Audit Management**
   - Security management
   - Audit management

9. **Enabling Support Management**
   - Managing people
   - Administrative tasks

Chapter 10

Refining the Hierarchical Matrix Model: Specialties and Roles

Management exists for the sake of the institution's results. It has to start with the intended results and has to organize the resources of the institution to attain these results.

Peter Drucker

In the previous two chapters, we saw that the design of the Hierarchical Matrix is based on a number of fundamental assumptions or tenets reflecting both strategy and human nature. One of the driving strategies for the design is to devise a structure that allows the cultivation of specialization organized around well-defined basic IT roles. The goal of this approach is to create a workforce with the high level of business and technical competence necessary for the organization to provide excellent and innovative products and services to its clients. We also noted that a major additional benefit accrues from this specialization strategy—namely, the increased ability of the organization to attract and retain the best technical talent because of more challenging work, supportive and invigorating peer work groups, and more opportunities to develop and expand technical skills.

In this chapter we further explore the implementation of a specialization strategy. For example, we explore the questions of which specialties should be developed and how they should be supported. We also consider the connections between the organization's specialties and its hierarchy within the Hierarchical Matrix model, and how the hierarchy supports the work of the specialties to ensure the proper balance of efficiency and effectiveness to produce the value clients expect.

Specialties and Specialized Skills

Before we can decide which specialties to develop and support, it is important to make a clear distinction between specialties and specialized skills. We will define a *specialist* as one who possesses highly developed knowledge and expertise in a specialty. While some specialized skills are often necessary, a specialty involves more than just a set of skills.

An analogy may help illustrate this point. If you are having a particular problem with your automobile, you are likely to seek out a specialist to fully diagnose and repair the vehicle. If you are having problems with your automatic transmission, you might prefer a *certified automatic transmission mechanic* to work on your car. But what does the phrase "certified automatic transmission mechanic" mean? It means a person who has acquired a deep knowledge and level of expertise in maintaining and repairing automatic transmissions. This person would then be in an excellent position to diagnose and deal with whatever problem might prevail with your transmission. A good portion of the knowledge and expertise that such a specialist possesses is different from the knowledge and expertise of, say, a *certified diesel engine mechanic*. However, these two specialists no doubt share a good many specialized skills. For example, they both presumably use certain automotive tools and various repair techniques, they know how to go about collecting and interpreting diagnostic data about an automobile's performance, and so on. On the other hand, each of these specialists possesses some specialized skills that the other does not have, and in fact does not need to have, to be successful in his particular specialty. The point is that being a specialist who is certified to repair a particular automotive subsystem involves a great deal more than just a set of specific skills. It involves both knowledge about and experience with the particular kind of subsystem in addition to any underlying set of required skills.

In the IT industry, the counterpart to a particular kind of automotive subsystem is a particular *process*. We have seen how the matrix depends on the use of a framework of integrated, highly developed, repeatable processes. These processes form the basis for specialties in IT. For example, one of the most fundamental processes in the IT industry is that of programming. People who have been educated and trained to write computer programs are referred to as *programmers*, which is another way to say that they are specialists in the process of computer programming. When they are described as programmers, others in the IT industry know what that description means. The specialty of programming is widely recognized and many educational institutions offer training in programming. Note that while the acquisition of specialized skill in at least one programming language is almost surely be a part of any such educational experience, there is more to that experience than just that component.

What do people have to learn to become programmers? First they must become proficient in logical thinking and problem solving, so they can translate requirements into algorithms and then translate those algorithms into programs in some programming language. To do this effectively, they must also understand the underlying model of how a computer operates as a finite state machine, moving from one state to another to complete its assigned algorithms. Programmers must also understand how computer programming languages can be used to represent algorithms in ways that allow them to be executed on a computer.

Of course, in particular contexts, they must also possess certain specialized skills. For example, if a particular programming task must be implemented in the language Java, the computer programming specialist must know that language. If, on the other hand,

COBOL is the language of choice for a project, the programmers must have skill in the COBOL language. But while skills in a particular programming language may be critical to the tasks at hand, they are not sufficient to make someone a programming specialist. Without other higher-level skills that form the foundation of programming, a person who knows only the details of the COBOL language would not be a valuable resource as a programmer.

By our definition of a specialist, it would be incorrect to refer to someone as a COBOL specialist, or a Java specialist, or an ASP specialist, and so on. The ability to work effectively in these languages is an *added specialized skill* that adds value to a programming specialist—that is, a person who has attained the higher-level logical thinking skills required in executing the *process* of turning requirements into an efficient and effective algorithm and then transforming it into a working program.

Let's consider one more example from the IT industry. We mentioned earlier that the industry had been slow to realize the value of the project management discipline to the software development process. But over the past decade or so, most IT organizations have come to consider expertise in project management a core competency. Indeed, the *process of managing projects* is now considered an important specialty within IT.

What are the skills that a project management specialist should possess? It is generally recognized that good communication skills—the ability to listen to stakeholders, discover and document their needs, and articulate project objectives based on these needs—is a critical skill area. The ability to organize, track, and monitor complex sets of interrelated tasks is another crucially important skill set. Even so, we don't ordinarily refer to someone as a "task organizing specialist" or as a "listening specialist," and so on. We seem to recognize that such specialized skills as listening and organizing tasks, while important, are components of the specialty. In a similar way, we must guard against thinking of specialized technical skills—such as knowledge of specific programming languages or tools—as comprising specialties. We should place them in the proper context as component skills within higher-level specialties.

Specialties and Process

A specialty then is defined by and tied to a particular high-level process. Specialists are experts at applying a specified process. Of course, not every process gives rise to a specialty. For example, we have earlier noted how important the process of escalation is within the Hierarchical Matrix structure. But that does not mean that we necessarily define the *specialty* of escalation and consider individuals to be escalation specialists. Neither would that possibility be ruled out automatically either. As we will see, whether escalation—or any given process—would be viewed as a specialty in an organization would depend on several factors.

First, as we have noted, specialties are focused on processes. A specialist is an expert—a person who possesses particular talents and knowledge—in applying a process. Usually, there is a natural name for such a person. For example, the terms *programmer, system analyst, project leader,* and *design architect* are suggestive of a person who possesses a set of skills and related knowledge about a high-level process. By contrast, it would sound awkward at best to speak of someone being a *listener,* an *escalation-ist,* a *task organizer,* a *presenter,* a *COBOL-ist,* a *Java-ist* and so on. These skill areas are not broad enough or at a high enough level to have a natural term to describe someone with the particular skills involved. Rather we would likely refer to them as persons who have good listening skills, good organizational skills, good escalation skills, and so on. This is another way of saying perhaps that the processes involved are not at a high enough level to be considered a foundation for a specialty.

Clearly, there is more than a little subjectivity in making such judgments, so there must be other criteria to help us better define processes as specialties. Perhaps most importantly, if a process is to be considered as a foundation for a specialty, it must represent an important component of an organization's work. It likely involves a number of different skills, and perhaps even a group of subprocesses. We might call it a *high-level* process. In most cases, such a process would not be peculiar to a given organization but would be recognizable and important to other organizations doing similar work.

If the process under consideration has all the above character-istics, it is likely, though not guaranteed, that the marketplace may have already given de facto recognition to an associated specialty. In this case, there is a good chance that educational providers have responded to the marketplace needs with programs to educate and train these specialists. Professional associations and organiza-tions likely exist to nurture the specialty, offering opportunities to network and develop professionalism, knowledge, and skill sets within the specialty. Such support mechanisms are important fac-tors as the organization considers how to populate and support the development of a specialty.

Important factors for an organization to consider in deciding on which specialties to develop are:

- What high-level processes are needed to support clients' strategic goals?

- What skill sets and knowledge are required for the expert application of these processes?

- Are such skill sets and knowledge available in the IT marketplace?

- What training is available or can be provided to support those with these skill sets and knowledge?

- How is the specialty supported and developed going forward?

In general, organizations seek to define specialties that the IT industry recognizes and for which educational institutions provide appropriate training. These factors make it easier to hire specialists—both experienced and new-hires—and reduce the organization's costs in training once they are employed. However, on occasion the organization may recognize and develop important high-level processes that are either peculiar to the organization or that would require deep knowledge of the organization. In these cases, a decision may well be made for the organization to provide the appropriate training, education, and mentoring to create a cadre of specialists.

An excellent example of such a specialty is that of design architect. While this term is recognized by the IT industry, it is unlikely that a design architect hired from outside the organization can become an expert design architect without considerable mentoring by those who know the organization's architecture, history, and strategic principles. It is important in such cases for the organization to understand the training and mentoring commitment that required to help such individuals to become productive within the design architect specialty.

Refining Processes through Specialties

In the previous chapter, we identified nine fundamental high-level processes that we believe define the complete process framework for any IT organization. But to be effective for a given organization, these processes must be refined to reflect the specific realities that the organization faces. This is usually accomplished by defining subprocesses appropriate to the organization's work and the specific ways it chooses to organize that work.

However, for the process framework to function smoothly, it must be integrated, highly developed, and repeatable. When new processes are defined, or existing processes are modified, the organization must take care to preserve these essential characteristics. The best way to ensure this is to develop a cadre of people who are expert at implementing those processes. For those processes considered mission critical, an excellent way to do this is to establish and support appropriate specialties. By developing specialties, the organization recognizes the importance of ensuring quality in its critical processes by supporting the development of experts at those processes. Not only does this approach bring focused expertise to bear, it also sets an expectation of excellence in process application.

The project management specialty provides a good example of the benefits of such specialization. Long before project management was recognized and supported as a specialty within IT, projects were being managed. The problem was they weren't always managed well. Those managing the projects were typically also doing other work—often the technical work of analysis, programming, testing, and so on. Given the lack of clear accountability for the management of the project (as opposed to doing the technical work of the project), it wasn't always recognized that mismanagement was central in the failure or under-performance of IT projects. Even when this was recognized, it wasn't clear how to improve the situation in a meaningful systemic way.

Recognizing the process of project management as separate from system development and establishing it as a specialty brought two critical changes. First, those charged with managing IT projects were given the training to develop the expertise and knowledge to conduct this process well. Second, once trained, these individuals were held accountable for applying their expertise and knowledge effectively. So when poor project management contributed to failed or sub par projects, there was a framework for accountability, which led to a natural process to implement improvements.

The establishment of specialties allows the organization to develop the appropriate organizational expertise to apply critical processes with consistent excellence. It also assigns responsibility and accountability to those within a specialty. When things go wrong, this accountability is the first step to understanding the situation before identifying and taking the appropriate corrective actions. A specialty and its organizational support also provide the context for improving the knowledge and skills of the specialists, which builds organizational competency and excellence in the underlying process. Finally, with the right organizational governance elements, the stage is set for effective process improvement for the most important processes within the organization's work flow.

Relating the Hierarchy to Roles and Specialties

We have described the organization of work around processes within the matrix itself. In addition, we have explored how the use of a framework of integrated, highly developed, repeatable processes makes it possible for the matrix to be a largely self-correcting system, usually operating with no hierarchy intervention.

Of course, the hierarchy operates with its own set of processes that supply the appropriate amount of management direction and controls to support the matrix. A natural question, then, is: how should the hierarchy be organized to facilitate its function within the organization?

At the high level, the organization of the hierarchy should be driven by the system architecture. We can view the system architecture as consisting of the two basic components of technical infrastructure and application systems, and we need appropriate organizational units to manage both. We should identify organizational units to manage the acquisition and maintenance of the infrastructure within the architecture and the acquisition and maintenance of the application systems being run on this infrastructure. Based on these identifications, we can assign responsibility to each organizational unit to be responsible for or participate in all or some portion of the fully defined, repeatable processes in the matrix based on the degree of administrative and operational processes to be implemented.

Before we address the issue of how to organize the hierarchy within these broad organizational units, let us identify more precisely the basic responsibilities within the Hierarchical Matrix model assigned to those individuals in the hierarchy. We can group these responsibilities into two broad categories: managing people and providing qualification to the framework of processes when issues arise that cannot be resolved by the self-correcting mechanisms built into the matrix. These two categories are related in a natural way—people apply the processes within the matrix.

To place the units of the hierarchy into a structure to manage people, we should consider how the people are associated with the matrix processes. These associations provide an excellent road map of the structure within the broad units in the hierarchy. The hierarchy must both manage people and qualify the framework of processes when this is needed. It makes sense, then, to organize the hierarchy so that those in it have the appropriate process knowledge and are also responsible for managing people who have developed expertise in those same processes. Within this general approach, it would then be natural to organize the hierarchy to manage people grouped by the various roles of the matrix processes. Note that from this point forward in our discussion, the word *role* indicates a person's association with one or more processes within the matrix.

We believe there are three basic IT roles that must be fulfilled as they relate to operational and administrative processes within the matrix: IT management, programming (application systems), and technical support (infrastructure). We also believe that the scope of these roles is based on the level at which IT administrative and operational processes are implemented within an organization, which is a function of the software used (developed or purchased), technology complexity, and staff size. Finally, we believe that people in a specific role must possess highly developed knowledge and expertise so they can be successful in their assigned responsibility and authority to apply mission-critical processes with consistent excellence.

An example illustrates this. For the project management role, the organization might create management units within the hierarchy, typically called project management offices (PMOs). The managers within a PMO then manage individuals designated as project leaders within the matrix. This doesn't mean that these managers are responsible for managing projects themselves. Instead, they manage the people or experts (project leaders) who manage projects. The scope of managing these experts typically includes such things as: hiring and firing; resolving conflicts; assigning project leaders; procuring additional project leaders when needed, perhaps by employing contractors or "borrowing" people from other PMO managers; scheduling vacation times; and enabling career path planning and development.

On the other hand, it would be expected that the PMO managers have enough knowledge about the role of project management to help resolve project-management-related issues that the self-correcting matrix cannot resolve on its own. For example, suppose the company has recently taken on a new kind of project work. Leaders assigned to these new kinds of projects may find that there are issues peculiar to this category of projects that consistently cause difficulties. In fact, it may be that the project management methodology requires adjustment. The managers within the PMO might then be called on to consider these issues and organize an effort to find remedies.

A PMO would also be charged with two kinds of ongoing quality reviews. Of course, managers are responsible for performance reviews of those they manage, so PMO managers would be responsible for conducting performance reviews of the project leaders within their assigned group. Second, a PMO would also be responsible for assessing the quality of the project management processes themselves and the way they are being applied. When these assessments reveal the need for training, professional development, mentoring, or coaching within the specialty, the PMO would likely organize this or at least make sure it is organized.

If the organization is small, one PMO might suffice for the whole organization. But in other cases, several PMOs may be required because the kind of work that the project leaders oversee may vary. The organization may need a PMO for the system development project work within the organization, another for research and development work, another for infrastructure improvement and maintenance project work, and so on. In this case, the PMOs are placed within the hierarchy devoted to the relevant kind of project work.

As another example, suppose the organization has developed a client management role. Advocates apply their expertise in managing relationships with specific clients. It's likely advisable to have a portion of the hierarchy devoted to managing client advocates. Once again, if the organization is small enough, one unit may manage all the advocates. But for larger organizations, several units may be required, perhaps organized by the type of clients they serve.

In summary, everyone in the matrix is fulfilling a role that can be associated with one or more processes. Hence this association principle can be applied to group people by their primary roles and the processes to which they are connected. Once roles are grouped this way, the hierarchy can accommodate the management of people in these roles.

Defining Roles within an IT Organization

To define the roles within an IT organization, it must determine the level of specialization it needs to efficiently and effectively produce client value. This is documented by cross-referencing the roles with the appropriate matrix processes and subprocesses and then developing a written definition for each role.

To help with the management of the acquisition and retention of IT human resources, it is helpful to understand the market value of each role. To obtain this information, each role should be cross-referenced to the appropriate IT resource marketplace job descriptions and documented, providing management with value ranges for each role.

To aid in the care and treatment of IT human resources, it is helpful to provide career development maps, which can help staff acquire knowledge in their current role or advance to new ones. Role-based career paths should provide individual growth opportunities for the staff.

Finally, to ensure that the IT human resources are available to meet the organization's needs, some type of position control system should be maintained. Every staff member is assigned to the primary role that they are currently capable of filling as well as any secondary roles they could fill. To aid the matrix in assigning available human resources, a work management system should assign qualified staff members to a designated role to complete a given work effort.

Constructing the Matrix Hierarchy: An Example

The I/S Division of BlueCross BlueShield of South Carolina has evolved a multiple-step process for deriving and maintaining the organizational structure for the hierarchy in a Hierarchical Matrix organization. The interesting thing to note is that the organization of the hierarchy is actually the last step in constructing a Hierarchical Matrix organization. We believe that the best way to organize management staff is to let the organization be driven by the architecture and the roles and specialties that must be managed.

All too often, the management organizational chart is decided early on, and the rest of the structure is derived from it. We believe that this usually results in disconnects between management and the technical workforce. The method we suggest should eliminate these disconnects and make management's job easier.

The following is a summary of the interrelated steps. This approach is intended to be used iteratively to modify and maintain the organization as necessary when important changes within the environment require it.

1. Identify matrix processes.

   Develop an internal framework for administration and operations based on internal experience and selected overlapping or missing components from best-practice IT industry frameworks to meet internal needs (the matrix). The IT process framework discussed in the previous chapter provides a starting point for this task.

2. Establish a system architecture

   Complete the identification, development, and use of a system architecture that defines the products or services that meet your clients' needs, how they are to be provided, what resources they require, and common components that can be leveraged across many clients.

3. Identify hierarchical structures.
   a. Using the results of step 2, determine the organizational units needed to acquire and maintain the *infrastructure,* which is a function of software use and technology complexity as documented within the system architecture.
   b. Using the results of step 2, determine the organizational units needed for the *application systems,* which are also a function of software use and technology complexity as documented within the system architecture.

4. Cross-reference the matrix to the hierarchy.
Using the results of steps 1 and 3, assign each organizational unit in the hierarchy to the highly-defined, repeatable processes of the matrix based on the degree the IT administrative and operational processes to be implemented.

5. Define IT roles.
   a. Define the specific IT roles required to accomplish the highly defined, repeatable processes in the matrix identified in step 4.
   b. Cross-reference the roles to the various IT marketplace jobs to ensure that market-driven value can be assigned to each role, and identify the IT market job families from which to hire.

6. Determine IT roles required in each organizational unit.
Comparing the results from steps 4 and 5, identify and implement all the IT roles required in each organizational unit to support the degree of interaction required within the matrix to produce the desired outcomes.

7. Create organizational charts.
   a. Using the results from step 1, create a chart showing the matrix processes.
   b. Using the results from step 2, document the system architecture.
   c. Using the results from step 3a, create an infrastructure organizational chart showing the relationship between the technical infrastructure and organizational units(s) responsible for the infrastructure.
   d. Using the results from Step 3b, create an application systems organizational chart showing the relationship between the application systems and organizational units(s) responsible for these systems.

e. Using the results from step 4, create a Hierarchical Matrix organizational chart showing the relationship of the organizational units in the hierarchy to highly developed, repeatable processes in the matrix and indicating participation or responsibility of the units in the processes.

f. Using the results from step 5, create an IT roles/matrix chart showing the relationship of the roles by logical grouping to highly developed, repeatable processes in the matrix and indicating participation of the roles in the processes.

g. Using the results from step 6, create a listing of IT roles by organizational unit and determine the number of staff required to support each unit.

h. Using the results from steps 4 and 6, create a traditional organizational chart showing the relationship between the hierarchical structure and the staff, which represents required IT roles.

8. Implement the Hierarchical Matrix organization and maintain it by repeating the preceding steps to accommodate changes in the business environment.

Part IV
Adaptive Change

Chapter 11

Change as Opportunity:
IT Governance and Quality Assurance

It is through curiosity and looking at opportunities in new ways that we've always mapped our path. There is always an opportunity to make a difference.

Michael Dell

In chapter 2, we discussed the advantages of evolutionary change and innovation as opposed to a revolutionary approach. The word *evolution* suggests a process of adaptive change. Adaptive change requires that the organization first recognize the need or opportunity to adapt and then apply an analytical and systematic approach to making the necessary changes. The foundation for a successful adaptive change process is the ability and temperament to see change as opportunity. If the organization has this foundation, it can actively seek the right kind of change—the kind that establishes the organization as a *change leader*, to use Drucker's term. In this chapter we investigate how some of the ideas we have presented so far can position an IT organization to effectively adapt. We also explore the value of including an adaptive change process group as one of the nine high-level processes in the IT process framework.

Recall that Drucker makes two fundamental observations about change: first, change is inevitable and second, any attempt to "manage change" is doomed to failure. But if managing change is not possible, can organizations at least learn to take advantage of it and position themselves in front of important changes rather than being swept along with the current? Drucker's answer is a clear yes, and he lays out four basic requirements to becoming a change leader:

1. Create policies to make the future.

2. Adopt systematic methods to look for and anticipate change.

3. Introduce change in the right way.

4. Balance change and continuity.

These four requirements are the pillars of an effective adaptive change process. Now we discuss the two aspects of a comprehensive IT adaptive change process: IT governance and IT quality assurance. As we will see, the governance system addresses Drucker's first and second requirements, the IT quality assurance system addresses the third, and the two together ensure that the fourth requirement is met.

IT Governance

In order for an IT governance system to be effective, the organization must first create a culture that encourages employees to think creatively and innovatively about what they do. The IT-OSD model provides a framework for developing this culture. It is important to realize that evolutionary change does not imply reactive change. Instead, to be effective, adaptive change must be proactive, anticipating the need for change and the right way to implement it. The IT-OSD model provides a framework for *proactive adaptive change.*

Both leadership and management contribute to and have obligations toward the development and maintenance of an adaptive culture based on the IT-OSD model, as figure 3.2 earlier illustrated. Leadership is more concerned with the vision needed to recognize and confront change driven by external influencing factors, while management is more in touch with any needs for internal process change. Once management recognizes issues with internal processes or policies that might require adaptive change, these would be handled through the governance system. On the other hand, the senior leadership team would typically scan the external environment on a regular basis. Based on such scans, they would then review the organization's mission, guiding principles, strategies, and goals and objectives, identifying any components that potentially need to be modified. Of course, when changes are required, these would not be made unilaterally but only after proper consultation and communication with the entire management team. Any needed changes in technical or management policy and practices is handled through the governance system.

The Hierarchical Matrix also encourages this culture with the systematic freedom it provides individuals to act within the framework of integrated highly developed and repeatable IT processes. Indeed, the matrix only functions properly when people understand and accept this freedom and associated responsibility. As we have noted, one of the most important features of the matrix is the fact that it provides self-correcting mechanisms that minimize the need for intervention on the part of the hierarchy, and the effectiveness of these mechanisms depends explicitly on this understanding and acceptance. Anyone working in the matrix should be able to submit ideas or change requests to the governance system.

With the appropriate culture in place, an IT governance system can provide both the opportunity for input about perceived needs to adapt and a mechanism for considering and acting on this input. The primary purpose of a governance system is to provide an orderly and systematic process for innovation and adaptation. To be effective, the governance system should provide for adaptive change in technical policy, process, and practice as well as management policy and practice—thus addressing the potential need for change in both the matrix and the hierarchy of the Hierarchical Matrix.

IT Quality Assurance

An IT quality assurance system works as a complement to the governance system. For example, quality assurance should work with governance to develop and refine the integrated repeatable processes with the matrix. The quality assurance system's scope in this partnership might include reporting and analytical processes that provide comparative measurements and other data to assist governance in evaluating the effectiveness of matrix processes. Quality assurance might also audit and investigate internal controls, processes, and management procedures of the hierarchy to improve the efficiency and general health of the IT staff and system resources.

When the governance system approves changes, quality assurance would typically be responsible for communications and training for the smooth integration of the changes. This includes working with governance on training materials, coordinating the training of management and staff, and ensuring that any related documentation is up-to-date and available.

The quality assurance system should ensure that changes are made in the right way, which has several components. First, every proposed change should be based on a documented need for change. Documenting needs requires assessment and analysis, which almost always involves gathering data and taking measurements. The analysis of the data and measurements should clearly demonstrate the need for change and identify the need's root cause. In addition, the quality assurance system should ensure that the change process itself is done well through proper communication, training, and ongoing support.

Balancing Change and Continuity

When changes are implemented in any organization, it is important to ensure that it is done in ways that preserve continuity. We have just noted that the proper implementation of change is an important factor in minimizing disruptions to work flow, which in turn will provide an element of continuity. But continuity can involve more systemic considerations as well. One of the most important of these is to consider potential impacts on organizational culture. Even apparently small changes can prove surprisingly difficult when they are inconsistent with organizational culture. Culture derives from accepted behaviors and in turn dictates the boundaries of what's acceptable. Culture can become so ingrained that changes to it are viewed as unnatural at best and perhaps unacceptable in more extreme cases.

Of course, it may be necessary to sometimes make changes that are inconsistent with the culture. When this happens, management should acknowledge the cultural shift, explain why the change is necessary, and communicate the projected benefits. Organizational cultures can be changed, but—by the very nature of culture—usually slowly and gradually. An understanding of this reality can ease the pain of cultural shifts and minimize a potential backlash. The governance system should include cultural considerations in any proposed change.

Another and potentially more disruptive outcome prevails when the changes being implemented are inconsistent with current organizational strategies. There are two broad cases to consider in this situation: In the first case, the organization is aware that a proposed change requires adjustments in organizational strategies. These adjustments must again be an integral part of the process of implementing the change. Recognizing these adjustments and communicating them effectively can minimize the impact.

In the second case when the conflict with strategy was not recognized and thus was not taken into account, the effect is likely to be more disruptive. The likelihood is reduced, however, if the organization articulates and communicates its strategies throughout the organization. But in complex organizations, it is not uncommon to see decisions that run contrary to underlying organizational strategies. Including a *strategy impact assessment* in considerations of potential changes can help prevent this. This should be initiated by the governance system, which may need the assistance of quality assurance to perform the assessment.

An example illustrates this last point. Suppose a problem has been identified and that the suggested remedy involves some changes to one of the highly developed repeatable processes of the matrix. Recall that one of the primary strategies within a Hierarchical Matrix structure is that the matrix should act as a self-correcting entity in the sense that most issues and conflicts can be resolved without requiring the intervention of the hierarchy. To enable this strategy, the matrix is evolved as a framework of delicately integrated, interconnected, and complementary processes. As a consequence, a change—even a small one—in one process may have strategic implications for the self-correcting capability of the matrix. Before the suggested change is made, it is necessary to consider possible process interconnections. While some such interconnections may be obvious, there may be others, perhaps second-order interconnections, that are not. An analogy would be the often-surprising impact a small change can have in a highly interconnected ecosystem. To prevent unpleasant surprises in the matrix structure, the governance and quality assurance systems must work together to analyze these possibilities prior to making the suggested changes.

Implementing an Adaptive Change Process: An Example

The I/S Division of BlueCross BlueShield of South Carolina has implemented a unified adaptive change approach. This approach is designed to create a climate in which change is seen as opportunity and adaptive change is encouraged and enabled. In this approach, the I/S governance and quality assurance systems work together toward these goals.

The division governance system consists of committees that authorize technical and management standards and practices. The Division has two governance structures, administered by two committees: The *Information Systems Standards Committee* and the *Information Systems Policy Committee*.

The Information Systems Standards Committee is responsible for technical policy and practice and is made up of representatives from all functional areas of the I/S Division. The committee and its standing subcommittees own the contents of the technical governing document, the Information Systems Standards Manual, which provides the organizations' development methodology, infrastructure, and work flow standards.

The Information Systems Policy Committee is responsible for management policy and practice and is made up of experienced management representatives. This committee and its standing subcommittees own the contents of the policy governing document, the I/S Management Practices Manual, which provides the management philosophy, personnel administration practices, and the approved set of repeatable processes.

The committees also work together to ensure that appropriate controls are in place around all highly repeatable processes. A person called the I/S governor is responsible for the functioning of the committees and is appointed by the CIO.

The I/S quality assurance system examines, evaluates, and analyzes the division's efforts to ensure that the highly developed repeatable processes, technical standards, and management procedures are working effectively to improve the overall performance of the organization. Quality assurance has responsibilities in three primary areas: compliance, measurements, and process management.

In the compliance area, it employs audit and investigational processes to examine, evaluate, and analyze the internal controls, processes, and management procedures. In the measurement area, it employs reporting and analytical processes providing comparative measurements of highly repeatable processes. Based on the results of the measurements, governance input, and compliance findings, the process management group works to develop, document, and introduce changes to the repeatable processes. The group also works with governance and the training department to produce appropriate training materials and coordinate the ongoing training of management and staff.

Chapter 12

The Learning Organization: One Approach

An organization's ability to learn, and translate that learning into action rapidly, is the ultimate competitive advantage.

Jack Welch

It comes as no surprise to anyone in the IT industry that change is perhaps the one concept that characterizes the industry best. The remarkable advances in computer hardware performance captured in Moore's law are indicative of the astounding rate of change that has been systemic to the entire information and communications technology field over the past four decades. Networking technologies have experienced explosive growth similar to that of computer hardware over the past several decades. When these developments in networking were combined with the remarkable security provided by public-key encryption systems, the Internet emerged as a standard business medium and venue.

While not advancing at nearly the same pace, the world of software development has nonetheless experienced its own period of substantial change over this same time period. One of the most fundamental changes has been the fragmentation of the field generated by a proliferation of software development tools, environments, paradigms, and languages. Compared to the much simpler software development of forty years ago, today's landscape seems daunting. Add to all of this the increasing integration and convergence of communication, entertainment, and computing platforms, and the rapidly advancing cultural phenomenon of social networking and you arrive at an industry awash in change.

The loss of stability implicit in these developments has placed our increasingly technology-dependent society and its institutions into a continuous process of transformation. Of course, the IT industry is on center stage in this arena. The simple truth is that we cannot expect a return to the stability of forty years ago in the foreseeable future. As a consequence, we must seek to understand, guide, and influence the ongoing process of transformation that surrounds us and characterizes our time. To accomplish this, it is imperative that we become ever more adept at learning—both as individuals and as organizations.

While many observers have recognized the need for all organizations to become *learning organizations,* this goal has proved elusive. Businesses are focused on strategies for competing in the marketplace; there is often little time and energy left over to transform into a learning organization—especially when the precise definition of that term is itself elusive.

Although we can offer no definitive solutions to this challenge, we offer some insights into a promising approach. As we will see, this approach is actually an extension of the specialization strategy we have previously explored.

What Is a Learning Organization?

There is no generally accepted definition of a learning organization. However, to give our discussion a context, we need to formulate a working definition. So we've adapted one given by Mike Pedler and colleagues:

> The Learning Organization is an ideal—a vision of what might be possible. It cannot be brought about

simply by training individuals; it can only happen as a result of learning at the whole organizational level. A Learning Organization is an organization that facilitates the learning of all its members and utilizes that learning to continuously transform itself. [31]

This definition recognizes that the learning organization is not a reality that can be achieved in total but rather an ideal to work toward. Indeed, we can never perfect or complete our own individual learning, and we often hear the phrase *lifelong learning* to capture this idea. So it would be unrealistic to expect this goal for an entire organization. Nonetheless, remarkable results are possible without perfection, and so the goal is to move the organization toward the ideal of a learning organization.

Of course, training and professional development are important elements of any strategy to create a learning organization, but as our definition notes, training alone cannot do the job. In Jack Welch's phrase at the top of this chapter, organizations realize the benefits of learning when they "translate that learning into action." Learning, therefore, must take place at the organizational level. The essence of the challenge is to translate individual learning into organizational renewal and transformation.

We believe that an essential factor in making this translation is to adopt and embrace *systems thinking*. This involves the ability to comprehend and model the organization as a whole, while at the same time identifying and examining the interrelationships among its various components. This approach to gaining an understanding of an organization has been endorsed by many observers of organizational behavior, and it forms the conceptual cornerstone in Peter Senge's "Fifth Discipline" approach to organizational learning. [32] In our view, systems thinking is the glue that fuses individual learning and organizational practice.

As we discussed in chapter 3, a practical way to embrace systems thinking is to adopt a model-based approach to organizational development. Defining and adopting such an approach requires a top-down commitment from senior leadership. Without it, attempting to create a model for the organization is likely to be unproductive.

However, once a model is in place and enjoys senior leadership support, it can greatly enhance the organization's ability to understand and articulate its mission, create strategies that enable that mission, and implement those strategies through processes and people to produce the desired results. Indeed, throughout this book we have used the IT-OSD model to illustrate the practical application of the model-based approach.

The model-based approach views an organization as a complex system. In Deming's words, a system is "a network of interdependent components that work together to accomplish the aim of the system." Recall also from our earlier discussion that Deming believed that most problems and opportunities for improvement in any organization are inherent properties of the system of the organization: "In my experience, most troubles and most possibilities for improvement add up to proportions something like this: 94 percent belong to the system; 6 percent are attributable to special causes." [10]

It seems reasonable that in translating learning to the solution of problems and the seizing of opportunities, an effective system model can play a crucial role.

A Partnership Approach

The primary focus of the organization is creating value for its customers. Certainly the effort required to create and sustain a learning organization is related to this primary focus—especially in the long run. However, it may be difficult to bring the proper numbers and types of people together to succeed in this because of two factors: First, this effort is not usually an immediate organizational focus, and second, the organization typically lacks the required expertise.

Thus, it makes sense to consider a specialization approach in which a second organization is engaged on a contractual basis to provide access to the required learning. This approach gives the organization access to those who specialize in research, teaching, and curriculum development in areas important to the organization's mission without adding the financial and managerial burden of directly employing these resources. And because the need for such experts changes as the learning organization matures, the contractual arrangement seems appropriate and cost-effective. Universities are surely one of the best, though not the only, potential sources of this expertise,

However, locating the appropriate expertise is not as straightforward as it may first seem. The expertise residing in a university or other educational provider is primarily at the conceptual level. While conceptual-level expertise is very important, its impact on the organization needs to be translated to the organization's particular industry, environment, mission, and strategies.

This observation brings us to the central guiding principle of the approach we are proposing:

> The expertise of the educational provider and the expertise within the organization itself must be brought together—blended—to make a successful translation from the conceptual learning level to the actionable level that will allow the organization to realize the potential benefits of an investment in learning.

This blending of expertise between the educational provider and the IT organization occurs when the two organizations form a partnership to enable it. It is important to emphasize that what is required is a *true partnership*, not just one in words or an "association" that might characterize a typical relationship. Further, each partner must commit to certain complementary learning and teaching propositions.

The educational partner must commit to the following actions:

- Acquire deep learning about the organization.

- Apply this learning to the creation of educational solutions for the organization.

- Engage in a *continuous* learning experience and relationship with the organization.

- Be flexible in applying the knowledge gained to address the organization's needs (faculty with industrial experience would clearly be a plus here, but such experience could also be acquired through sabbaticals or short-range employment).

The corporate partner must commit to the following actions:

- Teach the educational partner about the organization.

- Provide the personal involvement of senior management— the deep learning the educational partner needs requires this involvement.

- Facilitate a culture of learning by:

  - Embracing creative tension within the organization as a source of renewal.

  - Fostering open dialogue within the organization, making it safe for people to share freely and take risks in applying new knowledge.

- Use learning to achieve organizational goals.

- Value, recognize, and reward knowledge in the workforce.

Together, the partners must commit to the following actions:

- Establish and nourish an ongoing relationship of mutual trust.

- Develop a learning model that works for the organization.

- Work to refine the model over time.

The Learning Model

A learning model should explain the overall approach to be used in constructing and delivering the learning experiences within the partnership. The Paired Pyramid Learning Model (figure 12.1) we have created is a simple one, yet we believe it captures the essential elements of how individual learning of the educational partner can be translated through stages into actionable learning that can transform and renew the organization.

In the model, the first stage in individual learning is at the conceptual or general knowledge level. The concepts, principles, and techniques that apply to and help define the particular area of investigation are explored with general examples, exercises, cases, and activities illustrating the meaning and applicability of these concepts. This is augmented in the second stage by an exploration, guided by industry best practices, of how these concepts, principles, and techniques are interpreted and applied within the IT industry. At this level the illustrative components are replaced as appropriate with counterpart components that demonstrate the application of concepts, principles, and techniques. In the third and final phase of individual learning, the acquired knowledge is applied to the organization's context.

By the end of the three phases, individuals should have acquired a solid conceptual foundation for the topics under consideration, insights into how and why these topics relate to industry best practices, and some specific and concrete examples of how the new knowledge relates to their work environment. In addition, they have been challenged to think of ways that this knowledge might modify their own perspectives, behaviors, and tasks within the organization. Note that thus far, no one has been asked or given opportunity to actually employ this knowledge on the job.

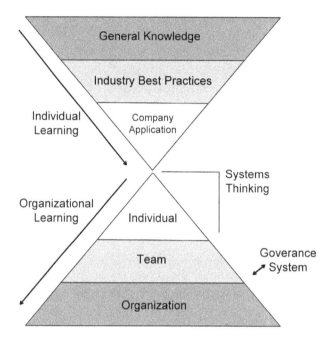

Figure 12.1: *The Paired Pyramid Organizational Learning Model.*

Once the three phases of individual learning have been completed, individuals return to their work environment armed with new knowledge about some relevant topic. In the first phase of organizational learning, they should begin to modify their own perspectives, behaviors, and tasks. Note that while this may involve no one beyond the individual, it is considered the first stage of organizational learning. They may in fact seek to share some of the knowledge with co-workers, but at this stage the main task is to find ways to enhance individual behavior and performance.

In the second stage, with the value of the newly acquired knowledge incorporated into the individual's perspective and job performance, opportunities may arise to share some of the knowledge with co-workers, managers, or those being managed. In this way, selected behaviors may be passed on to the individual's team. If a particularly good idea or technique emerges, it may be appropriate to submit suggestions for organizational change through the governance process.

In the final stage of organizational learning, the new knowledge produces modifications throughout the organization. Of course, not every individual behavior modification makes its way to this stage. Those that do have proved their worth not just to the individual but also to the overall organization. In this stage, the use of the governance system is essential in gaining an organizational perspective and assessment on the value of any suggested changes.

It is soon clear that the individual's path from general knowledge to company-specific knowledge in the top pyramid takes a much shorter time frame than the analogous path from impact on the individual's job performance to holistic organizational change. This is as it should be. But it is important to remember that improvement in individual job performance is a vital component of organizational learning and one that is more easily implemented than changes in the processes and procedures or that impact the whole company. Indeed, individual performance enhancement occasionally evolves into team or organizational changes over time. The governance process should be designed to recognize when these opportunities arise and shepherd the change process.

Earlier we claimed that the organization's use of systems thinking was the glue that fuses individual learning and organizational learning. Figure 12.1 illustrated the crucial point at which this fusion must begin. When an individual returns from a learning experience to the workplace with new knowledge, the system or model-based view of the organization can help the individual assess how improvements might be made in their work. The model-based view also enables an individual to be better informed when considering how these improvements relate to other parts of the organization. Of course, this view is also of great value in any larger-scope assessments of potential changes by teams and the governance system.

Becoming a Learning Organization: An Example

The I/S Division of BlueCross BlueShield of South Carolina has enthusiastically endorsed the concept and philosophy of becoming a learning organization. Since 1998, the division and Furman University's Institute for the Management of IT (IMIT) have engaged in a strategic partnership focused on the goal of transforming the division into a learning organization. The partnership has been guided by the principle stated earlier that the way to achieve this goal is to blend the expertise of the two partners to produce a successful translation from the conceptual learning level to the actionable level that allows the organization to realize the benefits of its investment in learning.

Both partners have embraced this principle and the complementary commitments described in this chapter that we believe make the partnership successful. The partnership has spawned programs like the project management and systems analysis certification programs we described earlier, as well as a host of leadership and management classes. But the program that best exemplifies the application of this principle and these commitments is the Post-Graduate Diploma Program, and most particularly the capstone experience of that program—the Summer Institute for the Management of IT.

The Post-Graduate Diploma Program is a unique program focused on the applicability and relevance of new knowledge, methods, and techniques in the management of information technology for today's business environment. It comprises post-graduate professional training in IT project management, systems analysis, and management and leadership skills. The completion of the program requires demonstrated success in the profession of information technology, the completion of a rigorous professional development program (a total of at least twenty-two full days of training), the completion of an integrative capstone Summer Institute, and passing scores on an examination over the core concepts of the program and a comprehensive examination at the program's completion.

We mentioned the Summer Institute at the beginning of this book as the primary inspiration for its writing. This capstone experience of the Post-Graduate Diploma Program is an eight-day residential program on the Furman University campus. The Summer Institute is an interactive experience with an emphasis on participants applying concepts in *their own environments*. During this experience, participants engage in intensive team activities, discussions, simulations, case studies, and scenarios that illustrate the application of fundamental concepts and best practices. The overall goal of the Summer Institute is to help participants achieve a high level of *integrative thinking and problem solving*. Topics are presented in a way that encourages them to synthesize this content when they are confronted with business problems within a technology company. Participants learn how to frame and define these problems, assess relevant information, consider alternatives, and ultimately choose good problem solutions.

The underlying theme of the Summer Institute is *IT: A Business within a Business*. Participants learn the fundamental skills and concepts needed to run an effective business, with application of these ideas to the business of information technology. The Summer Institute addresses some of the most challenging issues confronting the typical IT business, including:

- The economics of IT
- Marketing IT services and products
- Managing strategic client relationships
- Financial and cost accounting issues for IT
- Effective decision making for IT
- Negotiation and collaboration for IT
- Strategic thinking and planning for IT
- Innovation and creativity within IT
- Organizational design
- The Hierarchical Matrix organizational structure
- An exploration of the IT-OSD model

It is important to note that the collaboration that went into the planning for the Summer Institute did not end once it was launched. From the beginning, the CIO made the commitment to actively participate in the last two days of each of the institutes (there have been nineteen as of 2011). One of the LOB vice presidents has also been an active participant in the delivery of the financial/accounting module from the beginning of the program. Several directors have attended sessions specific to their areas of responsibility to add insights into the division's application of the ideas being discussed. In addition, Summer Institute faculty have attended management retreats and conferred with specific people within the organization to gain insights into how the concepts they teach are applied. So not only was the original offering codeveloped, but the ongoing development of the program has also been, and continues to be, a collaborative effort.

The partnership has produced a host of benefits to both partners. The benefits to the university are myriad. Of course the partnership has produced financial benefits, a portion of which the university has used to ensure the continuity of its engagement with the corporate community in similar educational partnerships. But beyond that, the interaction that the partnership has fostered has given a number of university faculty members the opportunity to see how their academic specialties can have significant application in the running of a successful company. This translates into new ways to engage university students in their classrooms as well as new areas for research and continued learning. As many observers of higher education have noted, this is just the kind of stimulation from the nonacademic world that university faculty need in order to relate academic subjects to the nonacademic world and provide the kinds of educational experiences that will equip their students to be successful in their chosen careers.

Of course, the primary benefits of the partnership accrue to the division as it moves toward becoming a true learning organization. Many of these benefits are naturally related to equipping the organization to maintain and improve its position as a market leader. But more importantly, becoming a learning organization means that the organization has the capability, flexibility, and adaptability to continue its success long into the future.

In summary, creating a learning organization is not accomplished by the application of a prescribed sequence of steps or the simple act of acquiring training. It is, in this regard, not dissimilar to the process of software development itself, involving as much art as science. In essence, it presents the challenge of the evolutionary modification of organizational culture, and surmounting this challenge—like putting Picasso on a schedule—requires an organization's best and most creative efforts.

Epilogue

Learn More and Get Involved

This book has explored a set of ideas and concepts that we believe are fundamental for the management of information technology as a successful business. As we noted at the start, these ideas and concepts have emerged from a ten-year collaboration between the authors, and their effectiveness is reflected in the remarkable success of a particular IT company—the Information Systems Division of BlueCross BlueShield of South Carolina. Though we have used examples from this company to illustrate the successful application of the main ideas, the book was never conceived as just a story of one company's success. Rather, it is our hope that anyone facing the challenge of managing an IT company, an IT unit, or IT projects of most any size finds ideas and concepts here that can help them succeed.

We believe strongly that in order to ensure success, IT professionals must be exposed to and institutionalize the common business practices and governance under which non-IT businesses operate, while at the same time maintaining a focus on technical competence. A major theme of this book has been to provide a conceptual framework that enables IT professionals to properly balance efficiency and effectiveness. We believe the concepts presented in this book enable this balance by offering IT professionals the ability to maintain and support the creativity necessary for excellence, while imposing appropriate structure and controls to ensure a balanced focus on technical and business competence.

Maintaining this balance has never been easy, but the significant changes that characterize the IT industry over the past few decades have made it even more difficult. These changes come from a variety of sources, including rapid advances in hardware, software, telecommunications, and associated customer expectations. However, there are two additional, and sometimes overlooked, sources of change for the IT industry. First, there has been substantial fragmentation of the software development field, demonstrated by the proliferation of software development tools, environments, paradigms, and languages in existence today. And, second there has been a diminishing focus on the need for IT professionals employed outside the IT industry within IT units residing as important subsets (what we have called "businesses within a business") of the manufacturing, transportation, insurance, business services and other sectors.

We believe IT professionals are important not only to the IT industry but that they are also essential to the success of the critical enabling roles that IT plays within virtually all industries and sectors. However, when discussing the career opportunities and the numbers of qualified IT workers needed in the future to fill those opportunities, the tendency has been to only look within the distinct IT industry, which ignores the 90 percent of all IT professionals employed outside the IT industry proper. Neither business units nor individual non-professional IT employees can control the data processing and process automation required to run a business efficiently and effectively without the help of IT professionals who are trained to focus on matching IT functionality and infrastructure to business needs.

This unsettled landscape presents unprecedented challenges for the education and development of IT professionals and leaders. In fact, we believe the emphasis has shifted toward a more narrow education about the expanding array of multiple, and often competing, technologies available, at the expense of an emphasis on two fundamentally important broader issues: (1) conveying a deep understanding of the unique characteristics of the IT industry, and (2) the application of solid business principles to the challenge of running IT as a business, whether in an IT company or in other business industries and sectors. Indeed, it is our conviction that the success of the IT industry depends on refocusing our collective attention on these two fundamental issues, and it is largely this conviction that encouraged us to write this book.

However, we realize that the successful implementation and adaptation of the ideas and concepts presented in this book depends on a deeper understanding than could possibly be conveyed in these pages. This realization has led to the founding of a consortium, with the explicit purpose of establishing and supporting a collaborative industry-university effort to encourage IT professionals to embrace the fundamental vision of running IT enterprises as successful businesses.

In early 2009, the Consortium for Enterprise Systems Management (CESM) was founded by BlueCross BlueShield of South Carolina, IBM, and the University of South Carolina. CESM initially focused on programs that provide ongoing education to IT professionals about the fundamental concepts of running IT as a successful business. As of the printing of this book, CESM has enrolled over sixty-five business partners and twenty-seven higher education partners in a collaborative effort to address this issue. In January 2011, the consortium introduced the IT-oLogy program to advance the study of information technology as a profession to a variety of audiences, including K-12 students, college undergraduates, new IT industry hires, as well as seasoned IT professionals and executives.

The IT-oLogy program provides opportunities through three initiatives: *Promote IT*, *Teach IT* and *Grow IT*. These focused initiatives drive real results by:

- Educating students, teachers, and parents about the opportunities available in IT, promoting the awareness of the need for an effective IT talent pipeline and its benefits.

- Influencing IT curricula with real world projects, internships, and the inclusion of IT professional skill requirements.

- Developing IT professionals and encouraging new ideas through networking and by acting as a broker for appropriate training.

- Enabling applied business research about the use and management of IT.

We encourage you to explore ways you can participate in the initiatives of IT-oLogy by joining CESM. To find out more and get involved, visit www.it-ology.org or contact Lonnie Emard, Director of CESM, at 803-354-5730.

Part V
Executive Summary

Chapter 1 Summary

Introduction:
The Art and Science of Software

Information technology (IT) is defined in this book as both a distinct industry comprised of IT-related companies and IT organizations within companies in other industries (i.e., IT as a business within a business). In either of these cases, IT is characterized by the following three components:

- The study, design, development, implementation, support, or management of computer-based information systems.

- The converting, storing, protecting, processing, transmitting, and retrieving of data for the following two purposes:

    - Data processing, which focuses on turning data into useful, meaningful, accessible information.

    - Process automation, which focuses on controlling machinery and/or processes to reduce the need for human sensory and mental requirements of work.

- The formation of a collection of products (computer or telecommunications hardware and software) and services.

Given this context, there are three main purposes of this book:

- To explore a set of concepts that we believe are fundamental for the management of IT as a successful business, either as a distinct industry or as a business within a business.

- To demonstrate that both types of IT organizations (distinct IT organization and IT businesses within a business) must seek balance between two competing fundamental objectives:

  - IT efficiency, achieved by business competence.

  - IT effectiveness, achieved by technical competence.

- To help educate business software users and purchasers about two fundamentally important issues:

  - The need for a more realistic set of expectations about software, software development, and the delivery of information technology as a service.

  - The insight to understand why they cannot control the data processing and process automation required to run their business efficiently and effectively without the help of IT professionals.

Two Major Challenges

Every IT organization faces two major challenges to achieve the desired balance between efficiency and effectiveness:

- Identify and adapt a complete framework of IT administrative and operational processes to provide excellent and innovative products and services to its clients.

- Identify and fulfill the basic IT roles based on the level at which the framework of IT administrative and operational processes are implemented.

- In order to better understand these organizational challenges, it is important to first understand the fundamental nature of software and software development because at the heart of every computer system is *software.* The fundamental nature of software and software development is a dichotomy—part art and part *science.* This inherent dichotomy results in important misunderstandings and misconceptions between business users and purchasers of software and those who develop software. Because software is an abstraction, business software users and purchasers have no intuitive frame of reference. There is no natural sequence of dependencies of software construction in the physical world that a person can observe and imagine.

- The IT community has attempted to provide a frame of reference by focusing on the science and engineering aspect of software development and leaving out the "art aspect."

- Recognition and acceptance of the inevitable art-science dichotomy of software development is the first step in both creating an IT organization that can effectively manage IT and in educating software users and purchasers to have a more realistic set of expectations about software and software development.

As shown in table 1.1, perhaps the best way to gain an understanding of this fundamental dichotomy is to compare the craft of the software developer to the craft of the artist.

Managing Both Art and Science

To formalize the management of the creative process of software development, there are three basic IT roles that must be fulfilled as they relate to operational and administrative processes:

1. Management
2. Programming
3. Technical support

The scope as well as the further specialization of these roles is based on the level of IT administrative and operational processes that are implemented within an IT organization, and this level is a function of the use of the software being developed, the complexity of the required technology, and IT organization staff size.

This book is about the challenges of managing IT organizations. Indeed, the art and science of IT organizations demands its own highly creative as well as highly developed and repeatable approaches to successfully manage its work. The essence of this challenge is captured by the metaphor implicit in the title of this book. IT work is in many ways the equivalent to putting Picasso on schedule to create a masterpiece that satisfies the following constraints.

- Be completed within a specified time period.

- Satisfy different art lovers' definitions of a work of art.

- Be delivered at "starving artist" prices.

Table 1.1

Art and Software

Summary of Similariaties and Diffferences

Art		Software
	Similarities	

Work of human imagination
Creative endeavor that produces "something from nothing"
Concrete realization of an abstract concept
"Requirements" change during creation
Incremental development
Creator has many degrees of design

Differences

Art	Software
No *a priori* definition of meaning, the "user" interprets for meaning	Created for a specific purpose and use
Different meaning for every user	Predictable, precise, and repeatable behavior and outcomes
Open-ended work	Schedule-driven work
Requirements are self-derived, exist in the mind of the artist	Requirements are external, exist in the mind of the customer
Created by a single artist—work of a single mind	Created by teams—the work of many minds, but should have the conceptual integrity of the work of a single mind
Process is unique to the artist	Process must be repeatable and consistent from person to person
Internal criteria for success	External criteria for success—decided by customer
No objective criteria or need for "perfection"; no measure of "mistakes"	To run, programs should be perfect—computer hardware demands perfection and acts as an unyielding judge of perfection
↑ **These factors do not require—would not allow—formalized management of the creative process**	↑ **For success, these factors require formalized management of the creative process**

Chapter 2 Summary

Evolution, Not Revolution:
Achieving Sustained Improvement

There are two basic approaches to becoming a "change leader."

- Revolutionary approach: creating drastically new and different ideas and concepts.

- Evolutionary approach: combining and adapting existing ideas and concepts.

An IT organization can best use an evolutionary approach to change in order to achieve process and product innovation that leads to sustained improvement, utilizing the following approaches:

- Recognizing that within current success lie the seeds of the great breakthrough of tomorrow.

- Being able to sense change and respond efficiently and effectively to it by viewing the right kind of change as opportunity.

- Determining the right kind of change by applying organized abandonment, insisting that the value of all work efforts justifies the associated costs.

- Employing an analytical approach to an evolutionary approach to change—utilizing the IT-OSD model, which provides a framework for external scans of the environment; assessing an IT organization's capacity for required changes, and aligning design choices to optimize outcomes.

Understanding Innovation

Process and product innovation can be best achieved when the true nature of innovation and invention is understood. Innovation is often thought to be akin to a "bolt from the blue." But in fact, it is usually the product of a more organized process. This process recognizes that innovation most often has the following characteristics:

- Does not usually result from flashes of brilliance.

- Does result from a creative combination of ideas, concepts, and products from existing technologies in ways that spark new technological innovations. (This is called *technology brokering strategy*.)

- Can sometimes be confused with the attributes of being clever or novel.

In the technology brokering strategy, analogy trumps invention when the following guidelines are adopted:

- Focus on recombining existing ideas rather than inventing new ones.

- Overcome the false assumption that the problem being tackled is unique and has never been studied or solved in any context.

- Assume there is a good chance that somewhere an analogous problem has been tackled and solved.

- Think laterally to help find appropriate analogies—think inside other boxes instead of attempting to think outside the box.

Sustained Improvement

Achieving sustained improvement can be enhanced by the following approaches:

- Leverage success by focusing your best resources on your best opportunities and not your most outstanding problems.

- Expect the unexpected, by recognizing that change is unlikely to be completely successful out of the gate and being willing to adjust as needed.

- Use the idea of "piloting solutions" as a vehicle for incremental implementation.

- Balance change and stability with the IT-OSD model (see figure 3.1 in the chapter 3 summary), which provides the following advantages:

  - Gives guidance in separating elements that can and need to be changed (specific strategies, goals, and objectives, organizational structure, and resources) from those elements that should be more stable over time (mission, guiding principles, and basic business strategies).

  - Creates the framework for communicating and understanding these elements to maintain proper organizational balance between change and stability.

Evolutionary Change, Competitive Advantage, and the Business of IT

A number of observers have endorsed the viewpoint that IT has become so commoditized that its contribution to competitive advantage is in question for most companies. We believe that this thinking is flawed for the following reasons:

- It does not recognize the constant efforts of business to absorb and integrate IT to enhance productivity and expand market opportunities.

- It has focused on the design and development components within IT that can and do produce commoditized IT components.

- It has failed to recognize that the appropriate focus is on the implementation, support, and management of computer-based information systems requiring the expertise of IT professionals to manage the data processing and process automation required to run a business efficiently and effectively.

We believe that efficient and effective management of IT by professionals as a successful stand-alone business or business within a business can provide competitive advantages with the following approaches.

- Using the IT-OSD model as a means of analyzing the degree of competitive advantage IT can contribute.

- Providing an opportunity for IT to contribute to the competitive advantage of the businesses it supports through an important category of software—*customized software*—for any client that has the following business characteristics:

  - The need to enable employees and customers to engage more effectively and efficiently in the company's business activities.

  - The ability to create a barrier to competitors through the evolutionary development of complex and difficult-to-emulate business intelligence.

Customized software can provide competitive advantage to clients with these characteristics by embodying a depth of business intelligence and algorithmic solutions designed at different points in time to perform complex core-business functions. However, the success of this approach requires the client's willingness to develop a strong relationship of mutual trust with the IT organization, enabling an intentional strategy of incremental development within a robust design environment that preserves the conceptual integrity of the system and the effective management of its increasing complexity.

Chapter 3 Summary

A Model-Based Framework:
The Information Technology OSD Model

Pursuing a strategy of ensuring the value customers need and expect must be intentional and provide the context for decision making across an IT organization. The key to implementing this strategy is to understand and articulate the integrated framework the organization uses to support the following elements of its environment:

- Work flow

- Decision making

- Accountability

- Adaptability

- Flexibility

One of the most productive approaches to understanding and articulating this framework uses the following approaches:

- Adopt the underlying premise that organizations are in essence complex systems.

- Assume that complex systems can be best understood through the use of a system model that abstracts the following elements:

- The most important features of the system.

- The major codependencies and interactions within the system.

A recommended system model for IT organizations is the Information Technology Organizational System Design model (IT-OSD model), which has the following features:

- Provides an evolutionary and systematic approach to IT organizational design.

- Enables extraordinary results to come from dedicated, but ordinary efforts of people, rather than looking to heroic efforts from outstanding people to create these results.

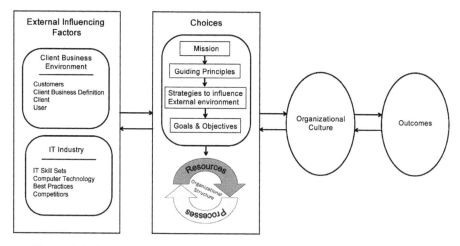

Figure 3.1: *The Information Technology Organizational System Design Model*

More about the IT-OSD Model

There are four major elements of the IT-OSD model, and each of these is explored below.

- *External influencing factors* represent outside elements that directly affect the nature of the results created by an IT organization. There are two broad categories of external influencing factors:

- The *client business environment* is characterized by the following factors:

  ○ The IT organization's clients, the clients' business definitions, their customers, and the users of the systems/services the IT organization delivers.

  ○ A client is anyone who purchases IT products or services directly from the IT organization.

  ○ The client business environment is defined by the buying and selling of goods and services by the client organization in support of its customers.

  ○ The client's customers are the persons or businesses that purchase a commodity or service offered by the client.

  ○ A user is any person who uses IT services for activities related to the client's business.

- The *IT industry* is characterized by the following factors:

  ○ Comprised of technology providers, the IT staffing marketplace, IT competitors, and IT industry best practices.

  ○ Technology providers are the source for computing technology—hardware, software, and communications infrastructure.

  ○ IT staffing represents the marketplace availability of the IT skill sets required to support computing technology used by the IT organization.

  ○ IT competitors are those IT companies that offer products and services that might appeal to the same clients that the IT organization serves.

- ° IT industry best practices offer frameworks in computer systems design, development, maintenance, operations, and management.

- *Choices* represent a range of important and related organizational design decisions that an IT organization must make—some explicit, some implicit—about the following organizational elements:

  - Mission

  - Guiding principles

  - Major business strategies

  - Goals and objectives

  - Resources

  - Processes

  - Organizational structure

The tables that follow give guidelines for making these design decisions.

Table 3.1: Guidelines for Deciding an IT Organization's Mission.

Design Decisions	Guidelines
Organization's Mission	

Identify and articulate the primary reason the IT organization exists as well as its distinctive competency. Long-term decisions should be considered in the context of the organization's mission.	To make this decision an IT organization must first ask and answer certain questions.
	• Is the organization:
	  ○ An IT business within the distinct IT industry?
	  ○ A business within a business, that is, an internal IT organization within a company within some other industry?
	• Is the primary focus of the organization:
	  ○ The creating, maintaining, executing and/or hosting of self-created systems?
	  ○ The selecting, installing, executing and/or hosting of vendor supplied systems?
	  ○ Some combination of the two?

Table 3.2: *Guidelines for Articulating an*
IT Organization's Guiding Principles.

Design Decisions	Guidelines
Guiding Principles	
Identify fundamental concepts and beliefs that drive the behaviors and feelings of those that work in an IT organization, who will ultimately make decisions (choices) concerning the ways and means the IT organization achieves its mission.	The fundamental concepts and basic beliefs are: • Used to find people who share these beliefs and principles • The basis for decision making rather than a set of ridge, narrow rules or policies More specifically, these principles should address basic beliefs about things such as: • Technology • Dealing with others • The organization's people • Effective communication • Effective leadership • Effective management • Values

Table 3.3: *Guidelines for Strategies to Influence the Client Business Environment.*

Design Decisions	Guidelines
Strategies to Influence External Environment **Client Business Environment**	

Acquire knowledge of the client's short and long range business plans, financial plans, organizational structures, and current business practices and operations to gain a deeper understanding of the business intelligence necessary for creating solutions to enable success for your client.
 	
Understand regulations, laws, and governmental entities affecting your clients and accommodate and perhaps modify regulatory constraints.
	Create strategic client partnerships by utilizing the following strategies.
	
	• Pursuing IT *solutions* and not just *products*
	• Effectively focusing IT organization resources on client needs and priorities
	• Recognizing that the high value a client places on the quality of the interactions with their product and service suppliers is the differentiator in deciding between suppliers with similar offerings
	• Implementing a *Client-Centric Strategy* based on:
	  ▪ The principle of *client focus*
	  ▪ Your system architecture
	
	See Chapters 4 and 5 for more details

Acknowledge the *IT Value Challenge* which manifests itself in an understanding gap between the client's intuitive-based perceptions and non-intuitive-based inescapable peculiar realities of software and the software development process.	First, address the IT Value Challenge through educating the clients about: • The client's personal but flawed experience of software and software development because there is nothing tangible for clients to "see" to give them the intuition, experience or knowledge they need to fully appreciate the nature of software and the software development process

	<ul><li>IT value measurement established based on the extent requirements and expectations have been satisfied, as jointly agreed to from the beginning of an IT work effort by the client and the IT organization</li><li>IT solution value which involves the proper balance between effectiveness and efficiency</li></ul> ***See chapter 6 for more details*** Second, address the IT Value Challenge by focusing on IT as a business both strategically and tactically by achieving the following outcomes.<ul><li>Strategic focus through:<ul><li>The Hedgehog Concept</li></ul></li><li>Tactical Focus through:<ul><li>Project management</li><li>Requirements management</li><li>Efficient and effective management of resources</li></ul></li></ul> ***See chapter 7 for more details***

Table 3.4: *Guidelines for Strategies to Influence the IT Industry Environment.*

Design Decisions	Guidelines
Strategies to Influence External Environment **IT Industry Environment**	
Major components of the IT industry include competitors, the IT marketplace, which supplies an IT workforce and IT technology, and a set of industry best practices. The successful IT organization must constantly monitor the industry and craft strategies to deal with changes and realities that emerge in that environment.	Carefully monitor competitors and specific products and services that are likely to appeal to clients. Ways to gain knowledge of technology providers are to: • Schedule meetings, conference calls, on-site visits, formal training sessions, and trade show attendance to keep abreast of technology trends • Review with a technology provider upcoming activities associated with their technology • Perform technical interviews and analysis with a technology provider to determine the road map/life cycle associated with their technology Implement or adapt IT industry best practices for efficiencies and effectiveness. Gain relevant knowledge of best practices by: • Monitoring leading professional organizations, associations, and consortia that articulate and publicize frameworks in computer systems development/maintenance, operations and management (e.g., ITIL, CMMI, PMI) • Cross referencing these frameworks to your own set of processes in order to identify gaps and areas for possible improvement

	See chapter 9 for more details
	Carefully track the definition and availability of staffing within the marketplace by: • Conducting compensation studies to determine skills categorization by IT jobs and salary ranges within the marketplace • Cross-referencing these jobs to specific levels of specialization of "roles" required by the organization to accomplish its mission *See chapter 10 for more details*

Table 3.5: *Guidelines for Establishing Goals and Objectives.*

Design Decisions	Guidelines
Goals and Objectives	
Determining goals and objectives involves identifying guiding and tangible milestones by which strategies are accomplished. These milestones should be specific enough to energize work and give meaning to strategies, and measurable enough that success can be established unambiguously.	Each goal and objective should be chosen to advance one or more of the organization's strategies. Thus, goals and objectives should be unique to a given IT organization and its overall mission and subsequent strategies, but to aid in their articulation, an example of such goal and its measurements follows: Goal: To attract, select, and retain outstanding professionals and provide them with the career opportunities they seek. Measurements: • Job offer decline rate • One-year turnover rate • Annual forced turnover rate • Employee progression statistics

Table 3.6: Guidelines for Managing Resources.

Design Decisions	Guidelines
Managing IT Resources	
We have identified three basic types of IT resources: • Application Systems: A group of interacting, interrelated, or interdependent computer programs designed for a specific business task or use. This is the face of the organization to customer. • Infrastructure: The underlying base or foundation (i.e., computing platforms, networks, operating systems, enabling software) required to implement and operate application systems. • People: A group of skilled IT personnel to build and maintain the application systems and the infrastructure.	To meet the challenge of managing its infrastructure and application systems resources, an IT organization should complete the identification, development and use of a system architecture consistent with and supportive of its overall mission. ***See chapter 5 for more details*** To meet the challenge of managing its people resource, an IT organization must: • Provide for the acquisition, development, and general "care and feeding" of the people • Define a set of IT roles commensurate with the level of the IT organization's framework of administrative and operational processes • Manage people within these roles so that they are successfully fulfilled in order to achieve the organization's mission ***See chapter 10 for more details***

Table 3.7: Guidelines for Implementing Processes.

Design Decisions	Guidelines
Implement Processes	
The successful IT organization must correctly identify and implement a highly integrated, repeatable, scalable, and complete set of administrative and operational processes that the organization can utilize to produce the required outcomes to meet its mission.	Using a process of adaptation from selected IT industry best-practice frameworks along with experience, we have articulated what we believe is a *complete* IT process framework, applicable to any IT organization, comprising nine fundamental processes distributed among three major process groups: Adaptive Change 1. Adaptive change process Business Perspective 2. Line of business (LOB) management 3. Client management System Factory 4. System architecture management 5. Application systems management 6. Service management 7. ICT infrastructure management 8. Security and audit management 9. Enabling support management ***See chapter 9 for more details***

Table 3.8: Guidelines for Deciding Organizational Structure.

Design Decisions	Guidelines
Organizational Structure	
To produce its desired outcomes, the IT organization must identify and implement an organizational structure that interconnects and aligns the organization's resources and processes.	An organizational structure called the *Hierarchical Matrix* structure offers some unique advantages to an IT organization. This structure: • Blends some of the most desirable features of the functional and strong matrix organizational structure approaches • Is particularly relevant to the challenge of balancing efficiency and effectiveness • Provides the IT organization the capabilities to operate with very scarce resources, while maintaining both the technical expertise and the flexibility to deliver excellent products and services to its clients **See chapter 8 for more details**

- *Organizational culture* represents the intangible "personality of the organization in action" as articulated in the mission, guiding principles, and strategies in describing how people are to behave most of the time. Culture has the following characteristics:

  - Culture is formed and changed slowly over a long period of time and requires great effort, skill, and patience.

  - Culture that helps retain good people is *not* the same as employee benefits that helps attract and hire good people.

  - "Bad" culture is a great barrier to organizational success.

  - "Good" culture can be one of the organization's strengths and competitive advantages.

- Outcomes represent the end results that define an organization's success, and we must have some tangible qualitative or quantitative measure of achievement of these outcomes to assess the degree of success.

Adaptive Change and the IT-OSD Model

To function effectively as a framework, the IT-OSD model must be flexible and adaptive enough to evolve. Overseeing this adaptation and evolution is the job of management and leadership teams. However, management and leadership activities are not the same, as explained below and illustrated in figure 3.2 (see chapter 11):

- Management focuses on activities that produce a degree of predictability and order. These activities are characterized as follows:

  - A set of processes that can keep a complicated system of resources (people and technology) running smoothly.

  - Overseeing the organizational structure and processes and the outcomes they produce.

- Leadership focuses on a set of activities that help direct, align, and inspire actions. These activities are characterized as follows:

  - Encourage groups of people to organize in the first place and guide them as they adapt for success in significantly changing circumstances.

  - Help create and nurture the organizational culture.

  - Provide the vision necessary to create, sustain, and modify as necessary the organization's mission, guiding principles, and strategies.

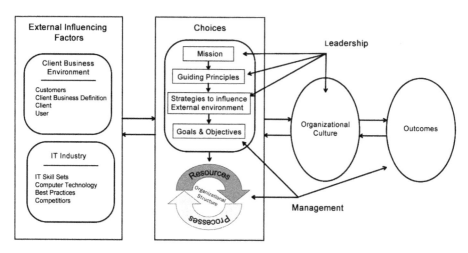

Figure 3.2: *Overseeing the evolution of an IT-OSD model for an organization.*

Chapter 4 Summary

Strategic Client Partnerships: Implementing a Client-Centric Strategy

An IT organization should create strategic client partnerships by pursuing a client-centric strategy to influence the client business environment. The following are important elements of such a strategy:

- Pursuing IT *solutions* and not *products*

- Effectively focusing IT organization resources on client needs and priorities by implementing the four C's of customer focus: coordination, cooperation, capabilities, and connections.

- Recognizing the high value a client places on the quality of the interactions with their product and service suppliers.

A strategic client partnership can be the differentiator in the client's decisions between suppliers with similar product offerings. To create this kind of relationship, the following approaches related to containing costs and limiting risks should be implemented.

- Leverage economies of scope.

- Understand gaps and deficiencies in current products and services.

- Leverage expertise.

- Share business activities.

Implementing a client-centric strategy requires two major commitments:

1. The client's willingness to:

    - Freely share essential business information and strategies.

    - Make a reasonable commitment to a long-term relationship with the IT organization.

    - Avoid assuming the cost and risk of getting IT solutions from an IT organization that does not possess sufficient knowledge about the client's business environment.

2. The IT organization's willingness to:

    - Operate with integrity in delivering honest value by being careful not to exploit or take undue advantage of potential lock-in strategies nor build in artificial or exorbitant switching costs for the client.

    - Minimize the risk of wasted resources being expended in developing IT solutions that prove to be insufficient to meet the business challenges for which they are intended.

A client-centric strategy is founded on two basic pillars:

1. The principle of *client focus*, which allows the:

    - Client organization to focus on the business problems, challenges, and opportunities it faces to succeed in its own business environment.

    - IT organization to focus on its expertise in providing outstanding IT solutions that are appropriate and cost-effective for the client's business.

2. The organization's system architecture, which supplies the capabilities to optimize the benefits of a client-centric strategy (see chapter 5).

Recall table 3.3 from the chapter 3 summary, which gives high-level guidelines for creating a client-centric strategy to influence the client business environment. Two primary guidelines are given there:

- Create strategic client partnerships.

- Educate clients about several important issues related to the IT Value Challenge, which is to create the proper balance of cost and quality for clients.

Table 4.1, which follows, gives more detailed information associated with each of the elements within these two major guidelines. Specifically, the table explores *what to do, how to do it, who is responsible,* and *who should participate* for each element of the strategy. The latter two factors are indicated by an "R" (for *responsible*) and a "P" (for *participates*) for the IT roles typically involved.

Table 4.1: More on Guidelines for Creating a Client-Centric Strategy.

Guidelines	What	How	Who (IT Roles)					
			IT Management	Client Management	System Architect	Project Management	System Solution Designer	Business Systems Analyst
	What to do	How to do it						
Major Guideline #1: *Create strategic client partnerships* **This guideline can be implemented through the elements listed in this column below.**	Value all client relationships, but spend considerable time and effort developing and nurturing partner relationships to help your organization reap the strategic advantages that are possible with trusted strategic client partners. For such potential partnerships, identify clients who allow you to obtain the primary strategic benefit of a deeper understanding of the business intelligence necessary for creating innovative solutions that enable success within the client's business environment.	Identify potential strategic client partners who: • Are themselves innovators and change leaders in their own business. • Believe in your organization's products and services, and recognize the value your organization delivers. • Are most likely to understand and appreciate the particular expertise and capabilities that characterize your organization.	P	R				

Guidelines	What	How	Who (IT Roles)					
	What to do	How to do it	IT Management	Client Management	System Architect	Project Management	System Solution Designer	Business Systems Analyst
Pursue IT *solutions* and not just *products*	An IT product is a system or service created to solve client problems from the *supplier's perspective on its own existing products or services.*	Use a product catalog, which is a listing of IT products (systems and services) that an IT organization provides to its clients.		R	P			
		Periodically compare the catalog to the system architecture to ensure the catalog's accuracy.						
	An IT solution is an IT system or service created to *solve client problems from the client's perspective.* A solution of value to the client must: • Address problems truly meaningful to the client—differentiating the client's outcomes from its competitors. • Achieve significant outcomes at a high quality and at acceptable cost parameters—delivering real value. • Be difficult for the client's competitors to replicate—providing competitive advantage.	Use a *Request for Solution Process* to provide potential solutions tailored for strategic client partners.		P	P	P	R	P
		Use a *solution improvement process* to provide potential improvements to existing solutions for strategic client partners.		R	P			P

Guidelines	What to do	How to do it	IT Management	Client Management	System Architect	Project Management	System Solution Designer	Business Systems Analyst
Effectively focusing IT organization resources on client needs and priorities—the four C's of customer focus	Coordination	Share client related information and decision making across the IT organization by establishing structural mechanisms and processes that facilitate activities and information flows across the various internal IT groups.		R	P	P	P	P
	Cooperation	Encourage all parts of the IT organization to work together in the interest of identifying and meeting client needs, and reinforce the behavior through appropriate metrics to measure and reward performance.		R		P		

Guidelines	What — What to do	How — How to do it	IT Management	Client Management	System Architect	Project Management	System Solution Designer	Business Systems Analyst
	Capabilities	Ensure that there are sufficient numbers of IT employees with the skills to deliver effective and valued client solutions and that clear career paths are defined for each category of employee. Such employees must possess the following attributes.	R					
		A deep knowledge of clients they are serving and their business environment to understand the clients' present and future needs.		P				

Guidelines	What	How	Who (IT Roles)					
	What to do	How to do it	IT Management	Client Management	System Architect	Project Management	System Solution Designer	Business Systems Analyst
		Knowledge and experience with the IT organization's multiple products and services in order to identify and assemble, if necessary, solutions of value to clients.			P		P	P
		The ability and knowledge to transcend internal organizational boundaries for the purpose of aligning the resources and expertise of the IT organization to address client needs.				P		P
	Connections	Leverage IT organization expertise in its own field and the set of relationships inherent in its segment of the industry to benefit its clients.			R		P	

Guidelines	What	How	Who (IT Roles)					
	What to do	How to do it	IT Management	Client Management	System Architect	Project Management	System Solution Designer	Business Systems Analyst
Recognize that the high value clients place on the quality of the interactions with their product and service suppliers is the differentiator in deciding between suppliers with similar offerings.	Leveraging economies of scope	Leverage the organization's development and support costs of products and services across multiple clients.		P	R		P	P
	Understanding gaps and deficiencies in current products and services	Ensure the organization listens closely to clients with the aim of identifying new products or product enhancement opportunities.		P	R			P
	Leveraging expertise	Act as a broker or synthesizer to bring key complementors into a partnership to create the appropriate IT solution.			R		P	
	Sharing business activities	Coordinate or combine business activities with the client to lower the client's costs.		R	P		P	P

245

Guidelines	What		How	Who (IT Roles)					
	What to do		How to do it	IT Management	Client Management	System Architect	Project Management	System Solution Designer	Business Systems Analyst
Implement a *Client-Centric Strategy*	Apply the principle of *client focus*.		Allow the client organization to focus on the business problems, challenges, and opportunities it faces to succeed in its own business environment. Allow the IT organization to focus on its expertise in providing outstanding IT solutions that are appropriate and cost-effective for the client's business.		R		P		

Guidelines	What	How	Who (IT Roles)						
	What to do	How to do it	IT Management	Client Management	System Architect	Project Management	System Solution Designer	Business Systems Analyst	
	The IT system architecture is designed to enable the successful translation of business strategy into technology strategy. The following elements comprise the system architecture: • Capabilities required to produce IT products and services that meet clients' business needs • Description of how IT products and services are to be organized and provided • Specification of what IT resources the IT products and services require • Identification of what common components can be leveraged across the needs of multiple clients	Conduct periodic review of system architecture to gain a solid understanding of its capabilities and the leveraging opportunities it provides.		P	R				

Guidelines	What	How	Who (IT Roles)					
	What to do	How to do it	IT Management	Client Management	System Architect	Project Management	System Solution Designer	Business Systems Analyst
Major Guideline #2: *Acknowledge the IT Value Challenge* **This guideline can be implemented through the elements listed in this column below.**	The IT Value Challenge is driven by a significant understanding gap between client and developer communities about the underlying and inescapable peculiar realities of software, and a disconnect between an IT client's intuition-based perceptions and the non-intuitive realities inherent in the actual software development process. *See chapter 6 for more details.*							

Guidelines	What — What to do	How — How to do it	Who (IT Roles) — IT Management	Client Management	System Architect	Project Management	System Solution Designer	Business Systems Analyst
Educate IT clients	The client's personal experience of software and software development is flawed because there is nothing tangible for clients to "see" to give them the intuition, experience, or knowledge they need to fully appreciate the nature of software and the software development process. The IT organization should help the client bridge this gap.	Understand what software is and how it is developed, and educate clients about its fundamental nature.		R				
	IT value measurement should be established based on the extent to which requirements and expectations have been satisfied, as jointly agreed to from the beginning of an IT work effort by the client and the IT organization.	Assist in the definition of work requests in terms of client business value utilizing data from a product catalog, and provide feedback upon work effort completion.		R		P		

Guidelines	What		How	Who (IT Roles)					
	What to do		**How to do it**	IT Management	Client Management	System Architect	Project Management	System Solution Designer	Business Systems Analyst
	Demonstrate IT solution value that possesses the proper balance between effectiveness and efficiency.		Encourage a proper balance between effectiveness (quality) and efficiency (cost and schedule) to deliver the desired value to the client.		P		R		
Focus on IT as a business both strategically and tactically *See chapter 7 for more details.*	Maintain a proper Strategic Focus: The Hedgehog Concept		Ensure that the IT organization is doing the correct work relative to its business goals.	R		P			

Guidelines	What	How	Who (IT Roles)						
	What to do	How to do it	IT Management	Client Management	System Architect	Project Management	System Solution Designer	Business Systems Analyst
	Tactical Focus: Project management	Complement the IT product development process (includes life cycle and methodology) by ensuring the development process can function efficiently and effectively through a set of umbrella processes that facilitate and enable tasks.		P		R		
		Ensure that the work being done is focused relative to its schedule, its budget, and its objectives (business goals).						

Guidelines				Who (IT Roles)					
What	**How**	IT Management	Client Management	System Architect	Project Management	System Solution Designer	Business Systems Analyst
What to do	How to do it						
	Ensure that the work requirements reflect the true work objectives, which are articulated at a level of detail and completeness that allow the system developers to build and deliver the required products and services.						
Tactical Focus: Requirements management	Intelligent management of requirements is accomplished using the following seven principles of requirements management: 1. Bad requirements lead to unsuccessful work efforts. Accept the fact that incorrect or incomplete requirements used to perfectly design and implement a solution will result in missed client expectations.					P	R

Guidelines	What	How	Who (IT Roles)					
	What to do	How to do it	IT Management	Client Management	System Architect	Project Management	System Solution Designer	Business Systems Analyst
		2. Requirements must be discovered, not just gathered. Accept the fact that most clients originally provide a set of symptoms that must be analyzed, identified, understood, framed correctly, and articulated precisely to ensure that the client shares the understanding, and then work diligently to capture requirements that ensure an acceptable solution to the client can be created. 3. Requirements discovery is a process, not an event. Accept it as an iterative process involving trial and error, which must be done over a reasonable time period.						

Guidelines	What	How	Who (IT Roles)					
	What to do	How to do it	IT Management	Client Management	System Architect	Project Management	System Solution Designer	Business Systems Analyst
		4. Good requirements demand client involvement because ultimately the correct requirements reside in the client's mind.						
		5. Requirements are never perfect. Exert a best effort within the time the work effort allots and move on. Avoid waiting for the perfect set of requirements to appear.						
		6. Changes in requirements are inevitable. Gain acceptance of a reasonable change control process with the client.						

Guidelines		How	Who (IT Roles)						
What			IT Management	Client Management	System Architect	Project Management	System Solution Designer	Business Systems Analyst	
What to do		How to do it							
		7. Develop a requirements partnership based on mutual trust between the IT organization and the client.							
Tactical Focus: 3. Efficient and effective management of resources		Produce the maximum value for the client. To accomplish this, an IT organization should operate as a resource-scare organization and deliver the results of a resource-rich organization. *See chapter 8 for a proven approach to accomplishing this.*	R	P		P			

Chapter 5 Summary

System Architecture: Foundation for the Value of IT

An IT system architecture has the following basic characteristics:

- It supplies the capability to optimize the benefits of a client-centric strategy.

- It exists for every IT organization, regardless of whether the IT organization invests in the effort to articulate and understand it and takes an active approach to develop and maintain it.

The system architecture comprises the following components:

- The capabilities required to produce IT products and services that meet clients' business needs.

- The description of how IT products and services are to be organized and provided.

- The specification of what IT resources the IT products and services require.

- The identification of what common product and service components can be leveraged across the needs of multiple clients.

The system architecture is designed to enable the successful translation of business strategy into technology strategy based on the following factors:

- The IT organization's understanding of the client business structure.

- Information exchanged between the client and other business entities in support of the client's business.

- The business systems required by the client to support the information exchange.

Software and Complexity

Whether an IT organization's mission is the creation, maintenance, and execution of self-created systems or the selection, installation, and execution of vendor-supplied systems, at the heart of every computer system is the software that supports the specific requirements of a given client.

Thus to better understand the use of system architecture by an IT organization, it is instructive to consider some of the fundamental characteristics of software.

Complexity is inherent in the development of software and does not grow linearly with the scope and purpose of the product being delivered. This is best demonstrated by considering the following four categories of software products:

- A program is:

  - Complete in itself.

  - Written often by a single author.

  - Ready to be run by its author on the system on which it was developed

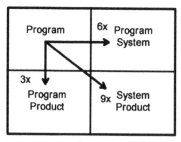

Software Outcome Types, and Estimated Cost/Complexity Multipliers

Figure 5.1: *Complexity/Cost multipliers*

and for the exact purpose the author had in mind when writing it.

- A program product:
  - Is a program that can be run, tested, repaired, and extended by other professional programmers for many different sets of data.
  - Must be constructed with a certain degree of flexibility and usability in mind.
  - Must be well-documented so that others can fix it, modify it, and extend it as the need arises.

- A Program system:
  - Is a collection of interacting programs usable in a *single* operational environment for many sets of data.
  - Can be run, tested, repaired, and extended by other professional programmers.
  - Constitutes an entire facility for processing large tasks and can be used by non-programming personnel in support of their routine tasks.

- A system product:
  - Is a collection of interacting programs usable in *many* operational environments for many sets of data.
  - Can be run, tested, repaired, and extended by other professional programmers.
  - Constitutes an entire facility for processing large tasks and can be used by non-programming personnel in support of their routine tasks.

The complexity described above emanates from the "thought-process" used in the development of software and increases over time. To properly manage this complexity, you must ensure three outcomes:

- Conceptual integrity within software that is developed by teams of many people by ensuring that the underlying design emanates from, or at least appears to emanate from, one mind or a small group of agreeing minds.

- Conceptual integrity within software that is modified and extended over time by increasing numbers of programmers, most of whom had no involvement in the original design and development effort, by ensuring that one mind or a small group of agreeing minds is always in control of the design being employed and that new components are designed within an appropriately constrained structure and set of possibilities.

- That as the users use the software, they clearly perceive the conceptual integrity and consistency of the user interface, which is ultimately the most important factor in its ease of use.

System Architecture and Complexity

System architecture is an attempt to make a computer system comprised of software that has inherent complexity accessible. This accessibility is accomplished by addressing the complexity that manifests itself in two fundamental forms:

- First, there is an *intellectual complexity* that is inherent in the system and derives from the following factors.

  - The complexity of the solution to the underlying problem being addressed by the system.

  - The scope or sheer size of the system.

  - The novelty or innovative character of the system.

  - The interconnectedness with and dependencies on other systems or components.

- The inherent complexities of the technologies to be employed.

- Intellectual complexity is addressed by making systems more understandable and intellectually manageable by using the following strategies:

  - Employ abstractions that hide unnecessary detail.

  - Employ unifying and simplifying concepts.

  - Impose a logical decomposition of the system.

  - Ensure the intellectual coherence of the various components of the system.

  - Ensure only the required minimum of logical coupling between different components.

- Second, there is *managerial complexity* that is implicit in the IT organization and the processes used to build the system. It derives from the following factors:

  - The complexity that may arise from the scope and size of the various projects and operational work associated with building and maintaining the system.

  - The communication overhead of dealing with large numbers of workers on such projects and operational work.

  - The interconnectedness with and dependencies on other systems or external entities implicit in such projects and operational work.

- Managerial complexity is addressed through careful management of the development of the system utilizing the following strategies:

  - Provide a natural scheme for decomposing the work needed through an architectural view of the system that not only makes the assignment of work more logically meaningful but also gives the various components of the work itself more coherence.

- Streamline and simplify the communication lines required for the management of the work to produce a clearer understanding of the various work product interfaces that the architecture can provide.

- Provide knowledge about, and access to, reusable components that can be leveraged to reduce the amount of actual work needed to build and expand the product.

- Direct and funnel software developer creativity into designing solutions that deliver value to the client by avoiding unconstrained degrees of freedom, which may lead to remarkable creativity in designing elegant and innovative solutions that fail to provide systemic conceptual integrity and reusability.

- Allow the organization to address issues that span multiple client organization boundaries.

A high-quality system architecture design addresses both the intellectual and managerial complexity inherent in a computer system through a logically coherent decomposition process that exhibits the following characteristics:

- Satisfies the principle of loose coupling between components.

- Is characterized by clearly defined interfaces, allowing the individual components to be dealt with in relatively independent ways.

- Links client business needs with the architecture.

There are two basic approaches to creating such a logically coherent decomposition process.

- A *business process-driven decomposition* has the following salient features:

- It focuses first on business processes to see how they produce outcomes.

- It analyzes how those processes match the processes modeled in a process-oriented system.

- This matching should be based on the interrelationships between technology, processes, skills, and culture.

- If this matching is poorly done, broad-based process changes within the business organization may be required to use the system

- A *business capability-driven decomposition* has the following salient features

  - It focuses first on business capabilities using a combination of people and technology, which is executed by business processes that support business core competencies.

  - It then moves to the technical design of those capabilities.

The capability-driven decomposition, as opposed to the process-driven decomposition, is our preferred approach because of the following observations:

- Different business processes might achieve the same capability, so business capability is the more fundamental entity.

- A system architecture organized around business capabilities has the following features.

  - It is easier for clients to understand which enables better client communication.

  - It makes it easier for the IT organization to map architectural components to client requests for new products.

  - It establishes a mechanism to directly link the system architecture to client business strategies, which in essence allows each new major capability to become a unit of design in the system architecture.

- It fits in the context of existing systems in order to enhance the value of past investments.

- It anticipates the future, incorporating known trends and likely future scenarios.

- It identifies and exploits opportunities for reuse within the system.

Managing the system architecture is done utilizing system architects—typically a small group of individuals who perform the following functions:

- Demonstrate through their experience and talents a particular prowess for system-level thinking and design.

- Make architectural decisions that protect and develop (manage) the system architecture by advising on those requirements collected and analyzed during systems development that:

  - Impact essential functionality of the system.

  - Have broad impact across one or more subsystems.

  - Involve significant development risks.

  - Make significant new performance demands.

  - Have the potential to impact internal or external system communications or synchronization.

- Guide the development of the system in ways that contribute to increased efficiencies, flexibilities, or competitive advantage for the organization.

- Help project teams become aware of more global issues that are not an explicit part of project requirements.

- Make broader architectural decisions that typically impact several different parts of the overall system and concern or impact system modularization, system performance and stability, global system properties, the fit of process changes with the system design, and system conceptual integrity.

- Take a system-level perspective to take such impact into account and to analyze the various trade-offs involved.

- Set the overall architectural vision, strategy, and fundamental design principles and concepts, chosen by the IT organization to provide:

    - A consistent approach and framework of a relatively small number of system principles philosophies and concepts.

    - A subsequent focus on reducing complexity and abstracting system characteristics, which in turn leads to the ruling out of certain design and structural choices and guides decisions and trade-offs among others.

Chapter 6 Summary

The IT Value Challenge: Balancing Cost and Quality

The realities of cost and schedule overruns and undelivered functionality, or at the least strong perceptions of these as realities, have created the following issues for the IT industry:

- They are clear proof that IT organizations face a serious value challenge with their clients, as demonstrated for example in *The Chaos Report*, a landmark industry study by the Standish Group.

- They have been written about, viewed, and advertised as a *crisis* in our software development methodologies and techniques.

- They have an alternative interpretation in which there is no so-called *software crisis*, although IT processes should continually be improved.

- They derive from a serious *understanding gap* between client and developer communities about the underlying and inescapable peculiar realities of software and the disconnect between an IT client's intuition-based perceptions and the non-intuitive realities inherent in the software development process.

In fact, clients base their expectations of the software development world on a number of reasonable but inaccurate perceptions that lead to this understanding gap. Their personal experience or *intuitive reality* is flawed because software development is based on a *non-intuitive reality*. This happens because there is nothing tangible for clients to "see" to give them the intuition, experience, or knowledge of what was involved in the process of producing working abstractions called a computer system.

The following table captures some of the major factors contributing to the understanding gap.

Intuitive "Reality"	Non-Intuitive Reality
Software development should improve at the same rates as hardware development as described in Moore's Law.	Software development is dependent on human conceptual capacity, which improves linearly (if at all), not exponentially.
Add more IT people if schedules fall behind.	Human conceptual understanding is the limiting factor, not the actual IT manpower itself.
Design and build systems "out of the box" that are fully featured and complex, and that satisfy all requirements both stated and implied.	Software developers, by the demanding nature of their craft, tend to be perfectionists, and this leads them to try and create software that satisfies all imaginable requirements, which in reality is counterproductive because the system need only deliver the *required* business requirements at implementation to be successful. The true nature of requirements is not known until the abstraction (software) is observed (either in testing or production) on the computing platform (the uncertainty principle). Note: Prototyping can help with this dilemma, but it only applies to a limited number of types of applications and features.
Solutions should take full advantage of changes in technology to be technically current at delivery.	Requirements should be written for a targeted technical platform and avoid frequent changes in technological directions to improve the odds of being delivered.

Intuitive "Reality"	Non-Intuitive Reality
All possible cases should be completely tested, and therefore completely error-free programs should be delivered.	It is impossible to completely test all but the simplest programs due to the different logical states that can exist. For example: a program with a total of thirty simple *if...then* constructs has 2^{30} possible logical states. If you double the constructs to sixty, then the number of possible logical states is 2^{60}, which is larger than the estimated number of grains of sand on all the beaches in the world. There is never a guarantee against logical errors.
Even small IT changes take too much time.	Logical coupling between program segments and components can occur inadvertently, often through the data used when a change in one part of a system causes unintended side effects in a different part of the system and requires effective regression testing to untangle the impact (the concept of entanglement).

Intuitive "Reality"	Non-Intuitive Reality
IT does not have a good estimating process because IT estimates are almost always less than the actual.	There are two kinds of cost in software development. The *cost of conformance* is the cost of meeting the requirements, which is more obvious, making it easier to estimate, budget, and monitor. The cost of conformance includes the cost of the creation process itself and the cost of planning, training, process control, process validation, design validation, inspections, walkthroughs, testing, and quality audits.
	The *cost of nonconformance* is the unanticipated cost of meeting the requirements, which is discovered as the project progresses so it is not estimated or budgeted. Because this cost is incurred during the project, it is harder to plan for and even measure accurately once it is incurred. It includes the cost of rework, scrap work, complaint handling, liability judgments, product recalls, post-delivery corrective work, damaged customer relations, and loss of customers.
	In fact, the cost of nonconformance in many cases exceeds the cost of conformance due to the following types of ambiguity in software development.
	• Creative ambiguity—There is much creativity involved in designing and implementing solutions that satisfy a given set of requirements, and this can lead to honest disagreements about the characteristics of a proper solution. • Communication ambiguity—Completely unambiguous, precise software requirements are fundamentally unattainable because of the communication gap which is unavoidable, and as a consequence there are often new requirements or at least significantly changing requirements that emerge during software development.

	• Clients are often unable to articulate precisely the requirements for their needs or problems because they describe their needs or problems in the language of the relevant business environment instead of the language of the system, which creates a natural and unavoidable communication gap. • IT organizations must translate clients' needs or problems into the language of a technical system that will be used to realize the solution, and not unexpectedly, the translation is flawed due to the communication gap. • At the heart of the matter is the inherent ambiguity and lack of precision in all human communication about abstract concepts; and software solutions are based on intangible, abstract concepts.

IT Value Measurements

Those features of a product (or service) that are required by a client should be measured. Such measurements should be based on the extent to which the *expressed requirements and expectations* of the client have been satisfied as agreed to from the beginning of an IT work effort, and should always involves some mixture of the major factors of cost, schedule, and quality.

Measuring IT solution value is not as straightforward as it may seem. The software development process is a creative process involving multiple developers all working with many conceptual degrees of freedom. This process must involve a proper balance between effectiveness (quality) and efficiency (cost and schedule) to deliver the desired value to the client.

- Striving for effectiveness, or quality, in a creative process has the following possible consequences:

  - This may lead to remarkable creativity in designing and implementing elegant and innovative solutions that satisfy a given set of requirements.

  - This may lead to differing levels of quality because the choices in deciding what quality level to implement are subtle and subject to interpretation and disagreement among those responsible for the implementation.

  - If efforts to achieve effectiveness are uncontrolled, this can lead to missed schedules and cost overruns.

- On the other hand, striving for efficiency in a creative process has the following characteristics:

  - It requires a focus on well-defined management processes for imposing the necessary constraints on the software development process to manage cost and schedule.

  - It should include the capabilities necessary to set and adjust priorities both among and within IT work efforts.

  - It requires a framework of orderly escalation of issues to guarantee the requisite product and process quality.

Chapter 7 Summary

Meeting the Value Challenge: Focusing on IT as a Business

IT organizations must balance cost (efficiency) and quality (effectiveness) to produce value for customers, which requires attention to the following objectives:

- Achieve and maintain a sharp focus against the natural tendencies toward resource dissipation caused by the difficult nature of software and the creativity of the workforce.

- Run the IT organization as a profitable business, whether a stand-alone IT company or business within a business housed within a larger organization.

- Support this focus on IT as a business by exposing IT managers to and institutionalizing the common business practices and governance under which non-IT businesses operate to gain competence in accurately measuring and communicating costs, which is a critical step in achieving efficiency.

- However, balance this focus on efficiency with a continued focus on technical competence, which allows managers to successfully manage technical operations and provide information for capacity planning and resource allocation.

Areas of Focus for an IT Organization

The successful IT organization must maintain a strong *strategic focus*. One way to accomplish this is to utilize the *Hedgehog Concept*, which has the following features:

- Is something intrinsic that is discovered over time.

- Provides a powerful insight to guide the development of strategies and the commitment of resources.

- Ensures that the IT organization is doing the correct work relative to its business goals.

The Hedgehog Concept can help the organization do these things by guiding it toward the following objectives:

- Avoid dissipating energy and resources on work outside the organization's excellence zone that will likely prove unsuccessful in the long term.

- Determine the kind of work the organization should pursue based on understanding three fundamental parameters that characterize the organization:

  - Expertise—the organization's fundamental knowledge and talent.

  - Passion—what the organization has a great passion for.

  - Economic engine—how to best use its expertise and passion to achieve and sustain economic success based on measures created outside the organization.

The successful IT organization must also maintain a strong *tactical focus* in the following critical three areas:

- *Project management,* which:

  - Complements and reinforces the IT product development process (includes life cycle and methodology) by ensuring the development process can function efficiently and effectively through a set of umbrella processes that facilitate and enable tasks.

■ Ensures the work being done is focused relative to its schedule, its budget, and its objectives for the realization of the IT organization's business goals.

■ Ensures that work requirements reflect the true work objectives and that these are articulated at a level of detail and completeness that allow the system developers to build and deliver the required products and services.

• *Requirements management,* which supports the intelligent management of requirements using the seven principles listed in table 4.1 in the chapter 4 summary.

• *Resource management,* which can be made both efficient and effective by:

■ Paying careful attention to the organizational structure of the workforce.

■ Choosing a structure that enables balancing the utilization of resources—which translates ultimately into balancing cost for the customer with the quality of the delivered products or services (see chapter 8).

The Hierarchical Matrix Model: Organization ModelValue and Scarcity

To produce the maximum value for its clients, an IT organization should operate as a resource-scare organization and deliver results as if it were a resource-rich organization. We believe that organizational structure is the key to accomplishing this formidable goal.

Centralized versus Decentralized Organizational Structure

There is no single best answer to the choice between centralized or decentralized organizational structures, but the choice should be influenced by an analysis of the following factors:

- The organization's mission.

- Client needs and expectations.

- Fundamental competitive strategies.

- Overall strategic goals.

- The system architecture's constraints and limitations on IT mission and implementation strategy.

- The form of the system architecture, though this does not provide a definitive answer.

- Distributed system architecture—*suggests* a decentralized structure.

- Highly integrated system architecture—*suggests* a centralized structure.

There are a number of common types of organizational structures that could be considered:

- *The functional organizational structure* is based on work being categorized into organizational units (often called departments), within which workers tend to perform a similar specific set of tasks.

- The *line of business organizational structure* is based on a categorization of work at a higher level than that in the functional structure, in which work is broken into units (often called divisions) that act as self-contained businesses.

- The *matrix organizational structure* is designed to bring together multifunctional teams assigned to projects or product development initiatives, but within which workers retain their respective positions in the organization to accomplish overall organizational objectives.

- There are three variations of the matrix structure, based on how teams are managed:

  - *Weak matrix:* A project coordinator or facilitator with limited authority is assigned to oversee the projects in this type of organization.

  - *Strong matrix:* A project leader is primarily responsible for the project and is held accountable for its success (most common form of a matrix).

  - *Balanced matrix:* A project leader is assigned to oversee projects, with power being shared equally between the project leader and the functional managers.

The Hierarchical Matrix: The Organizational Structure for IT

We propose a hybrid organizational structure called the *Hierarchical Matrix* as an optimal structure for an IT organization. This structure blends some of the most desirable features of the functional and strong matrix organizational structure approaches. It offers the following distinctive advantages for IT work:

- Provides the IT organization the capabilities to operate efficiently with scarce resources.

- Maintains both the technical expertise and the creativity to deliver excellent products and services to its clients.

- Offers a clear differentiation between the responsibilities of the technical workforce (the resources of the matrix) and management (the resources of the hierarchy)

- Provides the foundation for the success of the approach through the creation of a framework of integrated, highly developed, repeatable processes within both the matrix and the hierarchy.

The major features of the Hierarchical Matrix's two components are:

- The hierarchy is comprised of IT management, which is responsible for the following functions:
  - Supplying the appropriate amount of management direction and controls to support the matrix work.
  - Managing the acquisition and maintenance of the infrastructure within the architecture.
  - Managing the acquisition and maintenance of the application systems being run on the infrastructure within the architecture.
  - Managing people with a comprehensive system of acquisition, care, and treatment of IT human resources

organized by various specialties needed to apply the matrix processes.

- Resolving issues that arise that cannot be resolved with the self-correcting mechanism built into the matrix itself.

- Ensuring the quality of the infrastructure and the technical workforce itself and its efficiency in achieving the strategic objectives of the company.

- The matrix is comprised of the technical workforce, which is responsible for the following functions:

  - Providing the technical competence to ensure the effective and timely completion of excellent work.

  - Using adaptations of selected *IT industry best-practice frameworks* that correctly identify and implement a high-level integrated, repeatable, scalable set of operational and administrative processes.

  - Working within roles (or specialties) each of which is defined by a set of processes resulting in the creation of desired outcomes.

Fundamental Strategies underlying the Hierarchical Matrix

One of the fundamental strategies that the Hierarchical Matrix supports and enables is a *specialization strategy*, allowing the workforce to be organized into specialties (also called roles). The strategy has the following important features:

- This strategy leads to an effective technical workforce with increased technical competence.

- This strategy makes it easier to attract and retain the best technical talent by offering:

  - More challenging work.

- Supportive and invigorating peer work groups.

- More opportunities to develop and expand technical skills.

- However, the more people specialize, the more interdependent they become.

- Increased interdependence then increases the need for a framework of highly developed, repeatable administrative and operational processes.

A second strategy that supports the Hierarchical Matrix is an *adaptation strategy* that employs an appropriate adaptation of selected IT industry best-practices in defining an integrated framework for various elements of an organization's administration and operations (see chapter 9). The adaptation strategy has the following important features:

- It is important to realize that the various IT industry best-practice frameworks are independent, have overlapping and sometimes inconsistent components, and have particular strengths and weaknesses depending on the specific goals of the IT organization.

- As a consequence, adaptation, and not adoption, of IT industry best-practice frameworks is recommended.

- By adapting those components of various frameworks that are particularly appropriate, the IT organization can define a complete and integrated framework that is optimal for its own mission.

The *focused conflict and escalation strategy* is a critical success factor for the Hierarchical Matrix organizational structure. This strategy, through the features given below, is the mechanism by which the matrix component of the structure provides its competitively enabling efficiency and effectiveness.

- The primary goal of this strategy is to provide the matrix its own check-and-balance mechanisms to make it a largely self-correcting entity that can maintain a near-optimal use of technical resources with minimal intervention by the hierarchy.

- The strategy, in which the need to escalate arises out of conflict, can be viewed negatively because most people prefer to avoid conflict if possible.

- However, when properly understood, the appropriate kind and level of conflict should be viewed as a natural and positive outcome.

- The concept of focused conflict is built into the strategy for the following reasons:

  - Within the Hierarchical Matrix design, conflict is focused on the scarcity of resources and is inevitable within the IT framework of processes that attempt to optimize the use of resources.

  - Such conflict serves as the essential alert mechanism to draw attention to efforts that need some sort of intervention to maintain the proper balance within the work flow of the IT framework of processes.

- The complementary concept of escalation is built into this strategy to help resolve the focused conflict in a productive way, by accomplishing the following goals:

  - The primary goal of escalation is to ensure the timely resolution of tasks, issues, and decisions; assign accountability for resolution; and aid in identifying mitigation actions which cannot be resolved locally.

  - Escalation is built into the hierarchy to remove obstacles that are hindering the successful completion of work efforts and to resolve systemic issues or problems within the framework of processes and their inherent decision-making mechanisms.

  - Escalation should be viewed as collaborative negotiation, which is defined as a process by which two or more parties search for a resolution of issues that promote their common interest in the success of the organization.

- Proper escalation has the following essential features :

  ○ Escalation is not seen as a failure on the part of the escalator or the individual to which the escalation is taken.

  ○ Escalation should always be about work effort issues and never about personalities.

  ○ Except in emergency situations, use a "no surprise" approach before escalation by communicating that there is a risk or issue that may require escalation if not resolved.

  ○ Discuss risks or issues within the team to attempt a team resolution.

  ○ Once initiated, an escalation—even a verbal one—must be properly documented and actively monitored to track progress of the resolution, which, if not resolved in a timely manner, may require another escalation.

  ○ Escalation should be conducted as amicably and efficiently as possible.

  ○ Escalation should always focus on finding the resolution that best serves the goals and objectives of the IT organization.

Finally, the success of the Hierarchical Matrix depends directly on a strategy to create the right processes to support the work of the structure. At the high level, there are three components to this strategy (see chapter 9).

- Develop a framework of integrated, highly developed, repeatable processes within the matrix and the hierarchy.

- The processes within the matrix itself should contain decision-making procedures so that the matrix is largely self-correcting, meaning that a large percentage (ideally 90 percent) of issues that arise can be solved without the intervention of the hierarchy.

- Develop a metadecision process within the hierarchy to be used to investigate systemic issues that cannot be resolved by the processes within the matrix.

Chapter 9 Summary

Defining the Hierarchical Matrix Model: Nine Fundamental IT Processes

The success of an IT organization using the Hierarchical Matrix structure depends explicitly on a *framework of integrated, highly developed, repeatable processes* within the matrix and a *metadecision process* within the hierarchy used to investigate why an issue could not be resolved within the matrix. In additional detail, this framework should have the following characteristics:

- The framework should be *comprehensive*, meaning that it should encompasses all necessary work, thus providing the total context of the IT organization's work, and guide the individuals doing the work through various states required for success.

- The processes within the framework should be *highly developed*, meaning that they should have following characteristics:

  - Be complete when taken together.

  - Provide sufficient guidance for the work by being:

    ○ Flexible enough to allow sufficient creativity.

    ○ Developed thoroughly enough to provide guidance and basic principles that provide the thoughtful professional with appropriate boundaries for the exercise of the required creativity.

- Not specify or dictate all the work to be done in minute detail.

- Contain their own internal decision-making procedures, which require as little intervention from the hierarchy as possible.

- Instill into those working in the matrix the understanding and acceptance of the freedom and responsibility to make decisions and act on them.

- The processes within the framework should be *repeatable* meaning that they should have following characteristics.

  - Even though creativity is allowed, the process result must be predictable.

  - Repeatable processes thus enable the organization to avoid the chaos of *unrestrained* creativity.

- The processes within the framework should be *integrated* meaning that they should have following characteristics:

  - The processes must work together smoothly to produce a given result.

  - Clearly defined interfaces among the processes must be defined.

Nine Fundamental IT Processes

Guided by a number of best-practice frameworks for various aspects of the IT industry, we have identified *nine major processes* that encapsulate a complete framework of all required processes for any IT organization. These major processes represent a high-level view of this integrated process framework, and additional subprocesses can be derived by refining these processes into finer granularity. Of course, any refinement should be based on changing conditions and new insights and always reflect the specific mission, goals, and objectives, and driving strategies of a given IT organization. These nine processes can be broken into three major process group categories.

- *Adaptive change process group*—processes concerned with optimizing organizational change and monitoring and controlling other processes to ensure the overall quality necessary for the long-term success of the IT organization.

- *Business perspective process group*—processes concerned with building and maintaining the necessary client relationships and ensuring the effectiveness of the basic supporting business functions.

- *System factory process group*—processes needed to manage the production of products and services required by an IT organization's clients.

Supporting the process framework is an overall *metadecision process*. This process has the following characteristics:

- It has its own decision-making procedures that are used to investigate issues that occur within the process framework.

- It addresses the reasons the matrix processes that were designed to resolve an issue failed.

- It will determine which of the following two outcomes prevails:

  - One or more processes need some adjustment.

  - The difficulties lie in misunderstandings of one or more processes by those involved.

Following is a description of each of the nine fundamental processes.

The adaptive change process group contains one major process, the *adaptive change process*.

1. Adaptive change process

- Using critical assessments of the present, this process helps create the future through its two subprocesses, IT governance and quality assurance. These two subprocesses, which are described below, work together to fuel innovation and evolutionary change.

- IT governance provides for the orderly analysis of change in technologies, technical methods, processes, and procedures being employed within an IT organization as well as IT organization polices and management practices.

- Quality assurance provides for appropriate evaluation about the current state and performance of the IT organization, which informs an orderly analysis of potentially needed changes.

The business perspective process group is responsible for the financial management of an IT company or an internal IT organization as well as the overall management of client relationships within two major processes, *LOB management* and *client management*.

2. LOB management process

- This process is focused primarily on ensuring that the IT organization's products and services are provided in a cost-effective manner to its clients.

- The scope of cost management in this context includes the use of the three major IT resources of application systems, infrastructure, and people.

- Subprocesses are needed to ensure appropriate planning and budgeting, financial and cost accounting, resource acquisition, and contract management.

3. Client management

- This process is focused on building strategic client relationships and mutual trust.

- A key to building these relationships is enabling client focus, which allows the client organization to focus on what it knows best—succeeding in its own business environment—while permitting the IT organization to focus on its expertise in providing outstanding IT solutions that are appropriate and cost-effective for the client's business needs.

- Subprocesses are needed to ensure appropriate communication and coordination with clients at strategic, tactical, and operational levels.

The system factory process group is responsible for the set of six processes needed to manage the production of the products and services required by the IT organization's clients.

4. System architecture management
- This process is focused on the identification, development, and maintenance of the system architecture and the employment of management control processes to ensure the architecture's conceptual integrity.

- Subprocesses are needed to provide proper focus on the application systems architecture and the infrastructure architecture.

5. Application systems management
- This process is focused on the need for help from IT professionals to manage the data processing and process automation required to run a client's business efficiently and effectively.

- Subprocesses are needed to provide proper focus on the following needs:

  - A product development life cycle, which:

    - Defines the overall product development approach that will be used to administer all aspects of requirements definition, design and building or procurement of a solution based on these requirements.

     º Includes a system development methodology that provides a set of techniques and methods to manage the actual product development work itself.

- Project management, which provides an umbrella set of techniques and methods to manage the development work effort—stakeholder communications, planning, budget, and schedule.

- Ongoing support and monitoring, which provides a set of techniques and methods to manage the support and monitoring of the operational application system solutions required by a given client.

6. Service management
- This process is focused on the overall operational execution of IT products and services at a quality level corresponding to the objectives of a client's business and that meet the requirements and expectations of the users.

- Subprocesses are needed to provide proper focus on the following needs:

  - Service delivery, which includes service level management, capacity management, service continuity management, and availability management.

  - Service support, which include service desk, incident management, problem management, configuration management, change management, and release management.

7. ICT infrastructure management
- This process is focused on providing a stable information and communication infrastructure that is aligned with clients' business needs at an acceptable cost.

- Subprocesses are needed to provide proper focus on the following needs:

  - Infrastructure deployment management, which:

º Defines the overall infrastructure development approach that will be used to administer all aspects of requirements, solution design, and engineering (building or procurement) of a solution based on these requirements.

º Includes a deployment methodology that provides an umbrella set of techniques and methods to manage the actual infrastructure development work itself.

- Operations management, which:

  º Defines the processes related to the day-to-day management and operation of the ICT Infrastructure

  º Includes facilities management, scheduling, ICT infrastructure support, and output control.

- Technical support, which:

  º Defines the processes and functions that develop expertise about the current and future operational properties, systems, management tools, and configuration of the ICT infrastructure, which includes all computing platforms.

  º Makes calculations and undertakes analysis for capacity management and availability management inclusive of all computing platforms in consultations with change management.

  º Provides technical support inclusive of all computing platforms.

  º Provides the day-to-day management and maintenance of the ICT infrastructure inclusive of all computing platforms.

- Project management, which provides an umbrella set of techniques and methods to manage the deployment work efforts stakeholder communications, planning, budget, and schedule.

8. Security and audit management

- The purpose of this process is to control the provision of information, to prevent unauthorized use of information, and to provide support for audits of the IT organization by internal and external entities to ensure that the response required to an audit is accurate and timely.

- Subprocesses are needed to provide proper focus on the following needs.

  - Security management, which defines the needed level of security, taking into consideration internal requirements as well as meeting the security requirements specified in service level agreements (SLAs) and external contractual or legal requirements.

  - Audit management, which:

    - Defines the overall audit management approach that will be used to administer all aspects of discovery, planning, and conducting of an audit.

    - Includes an audit request methodology that provides an umbrella set of techniques and methods to manage the actual audit work itself.

9. Enabling Support Management

- The purpose of this process is to define a complete system of acquisition, care, and treatment of IT human resources.

- Subprocesses are needed to provide proper focus on the following needs.

  - Managing people, which defines a comprehensive program of general processes, programs, and information sources that are involved in effectively managing IT people assets.

  - Administrative tasks, which defines tasks required to ensure smooth operations of other internal administrative processes.

Chapter 10 Summary

Refining the Hierarchical Matrix Model: Specialties and Roles

Further exploration of the specialization strategy introduced in the chapter 9 summary produces a deeper understanding of specialties, skills, processes, and roles. The hierarchy should use this understanding to introduce refinements within the Hierarchical Matrix to ensure proper balance between efficiency and effectiveness to produce client value.

Defining Specialties and Roles

Specialties, roles, and processes are closely related. But while every specialty is focused on a process, it is not the case that every process gives rise to a specialty, as the following characteristics of a specialty illustrate:

- A *specialty* is defined by a highly developed, repeatable, mission-critical process.

- A specialty is associated with a process that:

  - Represents an important component of an organization's work.

  - Comprises a number of subprocesses.

  - Requires a number of different skills.

- A specialty is important to other organizations doing similar work and has:

  - Recognition from the IT industry allowing the organization to assign a market value for determining fair salaries for those practicing the specialty.

  - Support from educational institutions that provide appropriate education and training for the specialty.

The term *role* is used to describe a high-level task or responsibility that requires expertise in applying a specified mission-critical process. Persons fulfilling a role within the organization must have this expertise, and while this implies that they possess certain skills as well, it goes beyond just a set of specialized skills, to the mastery of one or more processes. Defining roles within an IT organization is challenging and should be guided by the following considerations:

- Determine the level of role specialization needed within the basic IT processes to efficiently and effectively produce client value.

- Cross-reference the proposed roles with the appropriate matrix processes and subprocesses and then develop a written definition for each role.

- For each role identified and defined, a cross-reference to the appropriate IT resource marketplace job descriptions should be created and documented, thus providing IT management with the appropriate market value ranges for each role.

- An organization should provide tools to help staff determine relevant training courses and programs to assist staff in strengthening and acquiring knowledge in their current role or in advancing to another role.

- Role-based career paths should be defined to provide a description of individual growth opportunities available to the staff.

- To help ensure that appropriate human resources are available to meet the needs of the IT organization, some type of position control system must be maintained in which every staff member is assigned to the primary role that they are currently capable of filling as well as any secondary roles they could fill.

- To help in assigning available human resources to work efforts, some type of work management system must be maintained in which qualified staff members can be assigned to fulfill a designated role for a given team assigned to complete a given work effort.

Constructing a Hierarchical Matrix Organization

The following provides a summary of the interrelated steps for constructing a Hierarchical Matrix organization:

1. Identify matrix processes.
   Develop a framework for IT administration and operations based on internal experience combined with selected overlapping or missing components from best-practice IT industry frameworks to meet these needs (the matrix). The IT process framework given in the chapter 9 summary provides a starting point for this task.

2. Establish a system architecture.
   Complete the identification, development, and use of a system architecture that defines the IT products or services required to meet your clients' business needs, how they are to be provided, the IT resources they require, and which common components can be leveraged across many clients.

3. Identify hierarchical structures.
   a. Using the results of step 2, determine the organizational units within the hierarchy required to efficiently acquire and maintain all or some portion of the *infrastructure,* which is a function of software use and technology complexity as documented within the system architecture.
   b. Using the results of step 2, determine the organizational units within the hierarchy required to efficiently acquire and maintain all or some portion of the *application systems,* which are also a function of software use and technology complexity as documented within the system architecture.

4. Cross-reference the matrix to the hierarchy.
   Using the results of steps 1 and 3, assign each organizational unit in the hierarchy to be responsible for, or participate in, all or some portion of the highly defined, repeatable processes of the matrix based on the degree the IT administrative and operational processes to be implemented.

5. Define IT roles.
   a. Define the specific IT roles required to accomplish the highly defined, repeatable processes in the matrix identified in step 4.
   b. Cross-reference the IT roles to the various IT marketplace jobs to ensure that market-driven value can be assigned to each role and identify the market job families from which to hire.

6. Determine IT roles required in each organizational unit.
   Comparing the results from steps 4 and 5, identify and implement all the IT roles required in each organizational unit to support the degree of interaction required within the matrix to produce the desired outcomes.

7. Create organizational charts.
   a. Using the results from step 1, create a chart showing the matrix processes.
   b. Using the results from step 2, document the system architecture.
   c. Using the results from step 3a, create an infrastructure organizational chart showing the relationship between the technical infrastructure and organizational units(s) responsible for the infrastructure.
   d. Using the results from step 3b, create an application systems organizational chart showing the relationship between the application systems and organizational units(s) responsible for these systems.
   e. Using the results from step 4, create a Hierarchical Matrix organizational chart showing the relationship of the organizational units in the hierarchy to highly developed, repeatable processes in the matrix and indicating participation or responsibility of the units in the processes.
   f. Using the results from step 5, create an IT roles/matrix chart showing the relationship of the IT roles by logical grouping to highly developed, repeatable processes in the matrix and indicating participation of the roles in the processes.
   g. Using the results from step 6, create a listing of IT roles by organizational unit and determine the number of staff required to support each organizational unit.
   h. Using the results from steps 4 and 6, create a traditional organizational chart showing the relationship between the hierarchical structure and the staff, which represents required IT roles.

8. Implement the Hierarchical Matrix organization, and maintain it by repeating the preceding steps as needed to accommodate changes in the business environment.

Chapter 11 Summary

Change as Opportunity: IT Governance and Quality Assurance

Evolutionary change is enabled by a process of adaptive change to achieve process and product innovation that leads to sustained improvement (value).

Here are some fundamental observations about change.

- Change is inevitable.

- Any attempt to "manage change" is doomed.

- By "adapting to change" you can avoid being swept away with the change.

- There are four basic requirements to "adaptive change":

    - Create policies to make the future.

    - Adopt systematic methods for anticipating change.

    - Introduce change in the right way.

    - Balance change and continuity.

Adaptive change requires an IT organization to recognize the need or opportunity to adapt and then to apply an analytical and systematic approach to making the necessary adaptations. There are two basic components of such an approach.

- An IT governance system, which has as its purpose to provide an orderly and systematic process for innovation and adaptation within the IT organization's administration and operations. It addresses the potential need for change utilizing the following methods.

  - It has oversight responsibility for technical policy, process, and practice (the matrix).

  - It has oversight responsibility for management policy and practice (the hierarchy).

- An IT quality assurance system, which works to complement the IT governance system by ensuring that any changes are made in the right way. It accomplishes this utilizing the following methods:

  - It provides comparative measurements and other data to assist the governance system in evaluating the effectiveness of the matrix processes.

  - It employs audit and investigative processes to examine, evaluate, and analyze internal controls, processes, and management procedures utilized in the hierarchy to ensure that they are working effectively to improve the overall efficiency and general health of the IT staff and system resources.

Together, the IT governance and quality assurance systems help create and support an adaptive approach to change. An adaptive approach to change encourages employees to think creatively and innovatively about what they do and supports a proactive attitude about change. Such an approach is enabled by the following characteristics:

- Leadership that provides the vision needed to recognize and confront change driven by external influencing factors.

- Management that monitors for the need for internal process change.

- An organizational structure (the Hierarchical Matrix) that provides the systematic freedom for individuals to act through their understanding and acceptance of their individual roles and responsibilities.

- The preservation of the continuity of the IT organization to minimize disruptions by ensuring that any proposed changes are smoothly integrated into the IT organization's overall culture.

- Established behaviors that dictate the boundaries of what is acceptable change within an organization.

Chapter 12 Summary

The Learning Organization: One Approach

Change is the one concept that perhaps characterizes the IT industry best. Over the past few decades, significant changes have occurred in the following core IT areas:

- Infrastructure—computer hardware performance, networking technologies, public-key encryption systems, the Internet as a business medium and venue.

- Software development—the fragmentation of the field generated by a proliferation of software development tools and environments, paradigms, and languages.

- Integration—the convergence in communication, entertainment, computing platforms, and social networking.

Changes of the magnitude that have occurred in these areas have caused a serious loss of stability by placing our increasingly technology-dependent society and its institutions into a continuous process of transformation for the foreseeable future. To combat this loss of stability it is imperative that we become more adept at *learning*—both as individuals and organizations.

Our Approach to Becoming a Learning Organization

While many observers have recognized the need for all organizations to become learning organizations to address the continuous process of transformation they face, the achievement of this goal has proven elusive. Although we can offer no definitive solutions for this challenge, we do offer a particular approach that we believe offers great promise.

A learning organization can be defined as follows.

> The *learning organization* is an ideal—a vision of what might be possible. It cannot be brought about simply by training individuals; it can only happen as a result of learning at the whole organizational level. A learning organization is an one that facilitates the learning of all its members and uses that learning to continuously transform itself.

The following table summarizes our particular approach by comparing the challenges and possible solutions to move an organization toward the ideal of a learning organization.

Challenge	Solution
A learning organization is not a reality that can be achieved in total.	Recognize that if we never perfect or complete our own individual learning, it is unrealistic to expect to do so for an entire organization; as with an individual, the organization will be a *lifelong learner.*
Translate individual learning into organizational renewal and transformation.	• Embrace systems thinking, which involves the ability to comprehend and model the organization as a whole while at the same time identifying and examining the interrelationships among its various components. • Adopt systems thinking through the practical application of the model approach to IT organizational development utilizing the IT-OSD model.

Challenge	Solution

Recognize that creating and sustaining a learning organization is (1) not usually an immediate organizational focus, and (2) the organization typically lacks the required learning/teaching expertise.	Use a partnership approach with the following features:
	• The expertise of the educational provider and the expertise within the organization itself must be brought together—blended—to make a successful translation from the conceptual learning level to the actionable level that will allow the organization to realize the potential benefits of an investment in learning.
	• The educational partner must commit to the following propositions:
	  • Acquire deep learning about the organization.
	  • Apply this learning to the creation of educational solutions for the organization.
	  • Engage in a *continuous* learning experience and relationship with the organization.
	  • Be flexible in applying the knowledge gained to address the organization's needs.
	
	• The corporate partner must commit to the following propositions:
	  • Teach the educational partner about the organization.
	  • Provide the personal involvement of senior management—the deep learning the educational partner needs requires this involvement.

Challenge	Solution

	• Facilitate a culture of learning by:
	  ◦ Embracing creative tension within the organization as a source of renewal.
	  ◦ Fostering open dialogue within the organization, and making it safe for people to share freely and take risks in applying new knowledge.
	  ◦ Using learning to achieve organizational goals.
	  ◦ Valuing, recognizing, and rewarding knowledge in its workforce.
	
	• Together, the partners must commit to the following propositions:
	  • Establish and nourish an ongoing relationship of mutual trust.
	  • Develop a learning model that works for the organization.
	  • Work to refine the model over time.

Challenge	Solution
Devise the overall approach to be used in constructing and delivering the learning experience within the partnership approach to creating a learning organization.	Use the Paired Pyramid Learning Model, which has the following components: • Individual learning levels: • Conceptual or general knowledge level—concepts, principles, and techniques that apply to and help define a particular area of investigation are explored. • Industry best practices—an exploration, guided by industry best practices, of how these concepts, principles, and techniques are interpreted and applied within the IT industry. • Company application—the acquired knowledge is applied to the organization's context, as ways that the knowledge and best practices might be applied within the particular organization's environment are explored. • Organizational learning levels: • Individual—take up the challenge of using the newly acquired knowledge to begin to modify an individual's own perspectives, behaviors, and tasks. • Team—share some of the newly incorporated knowledge with coworkers, managers, or those being managed, thus passing on selected behaviors to team members.

Challenge	Solution
	• Organization—although not every individual's newfound knowledge results in suggested modifications in the larger organization, for those that do, the use of the governance system is essential in gaining an organizational perspective and assessment on the value of any suggested changes. Systems thinking (IT-OSD model view) is the glue that helps fuse individual learning and organizational learning. It accomplishes this by the following methods: • Helping in the individual's assessment of the context within which any suggested modifications to organization might be made in their scope of work. • Allowing an individual to be better informed when considering how these modifications might scale or relate to other interconnected parts of the organization. • Aiding teams and the governance system in larger-scope assessments of potential modifications.

Endnotes

1. Frederick P. Brooks, Jr., *The Mythical Man-Month: Essays on Software Engineering, Silver Anniversary Edition* (Boston: Addison-Wesley, 1995).
2. Donald Knuth, *The Art of Computer Programming*, 3rd Ed. (Reading, MA: Addison-Wesley, 1998).
3. Peter Drucker, *Management Challenges for the 21st Century* (New York: Harper Business, 1999).
4. Jim Collins, *Good to Great* (New York: Harper Business, 2001).
5. Andrew Hargadon, *How Breakthroughs Happen: The Surprising Truth about How Companies Innovate* (Boston: Harvard Business Press, 2003).
6. Andrew Hargadon, "The Trouble with Out-of-the-Box Thinking," *ACM Ubiquity.* (www.ate.co.nz/innovation/hargadon.html, accessed 1/8/2012).
7. Edward DeBono, *Lateral Thinking: Creativity Step by Step* (New York: Harper, 1973).
8. Nicholas Carr, "IT Doesn't Matter," *Harvard Business Review* 81, (May, 2003).
9. Michael Masnick, "Nanotech Excitement Boosts Wrong Stock." (www.techdirt.com/articles/20031204/0824235. shtm).
10. W. Edwards Deming, *The New Economics for Government, Industry, and Education,* 2nd Ed. (Boston: MIT Press, 2000).
11. Paul Gustavson, "Our [OPD] Methodology," (www.organizationdesign.com/_productsAndServices.html, accessed 1/8/2012).
12. Project Management Institute, *A Guide to the Project Management Body of Knowledge,* 4th Ed., (Newtown Square, PA: Project Management Institute, 2008).

13. Michael Porter, "What is Strategy?" *Harvard Business Review* 74 (November/December 1996).

14. Ranjay Gulati, "Silo Busting: How to Execute on the Promise of Customer Focus," *Harvard Business Review* 85 (May 2007).

15. Mark Vandenbosch and Nijar Dawar, "Beyond Better Products: Capturing Value in Customer Interactions," *MIT Sloan Business Review* 43, no. 4 (2002).

16. IEEE Standard 610.12-1990: *IEEE Standard Glossary of Software Engineering Terminology* (New York: 1990).

17. David Garlan and Dewayne Perry, "Introduction to the Special Issue on Software Architecture," *IEEE Transactions on Software Engineering* 21, no. 4 (1995).

18. *Merriam-Webster's Collegiate Dictionary* (www.merriam-webster.com/dictionary/architectural, accessed 1/8/2012).

19. Alexander Drobik, "Enterprise Architecture: The Business Issues and Drivers," (www.gartner.com/DisplayDocument?id=366199, accessed 1/8/2012).

20. Grady Booch, Ivar Jacobsen, and Jim Rumbaugh, Interview in *IEEE Computer Magazine* 29, no. 5 (May 1996).

21. Dana Bredemeyer and Ruth Malan, "Software Architecture: Central Concerns, Key Decisions," (www.bredemeyer.com/pdf_files/ArchitectureDefinition.PDF, accessed 1/8/2012).

22. Joe Batman, "Characteristics of an Organization with Mature Architecture Practices," *Essays on Software Architecture* (SEI, Carnegie Mellon University, Pittsburgh, PA, 1993).

23. *Standish Group CHAOS Report* (www.projectsmart.co.uk/docs/chaos-report.pdf, accessed 1/8/2012).

24. *ISO 9000 Quality Standard* (www.iso.org/iso/iso_catalogue/management_and_leadership_standards/quality_management/qmp.htm, accessed 1/8/2012).

25. Philip Crosby, *Quality Is Free: The Art of Making Quality Certain* (New York: McGraw-Hill, 1980),

26. Barry Boehm, *Software Economics* (Upper Saddle River, NJ: Prentice-Hall, 1981).

27. Arthur Stephenson, et al., "Mars Climate Orbiter Mishap Investigation Board Phase I Report," (ftp://ftp.hq.nasa.

gov/pub/pao/reports/1999/MCO_report.pdf, accessed 1/8/2012).

28. Gordon Moore, "Cramming More Components onto Integrated Circuits," *Electronics Magazine* 38, no. 8(1965).

29. Clayton Christensen, *The Innovator's Dilemma*, (Boston: Harvard Business Press, 1997)

30. Ludvik Kowalski and Howard McAllister, "Estimate the Number of Grains of Sand on All the Beaches of the Earth." (www.hawaii.edu/suremath/jsand.html, accessed 1/8/2012).

31. Mike Pedler, John Burgoyne, and Tom Boydell, *The Learning Company: A Strategy for Sustainable Development* (New York: McGraw-Hill, 1996)

32. Peter Senge, *The Fifth Discipline: The Art and Practice of the Learning Organization* (New York: Doubleday Business, 1994).